A SOUND APPROACH

A SOUND APPROACH

Using Phonemic Awareness to Teach Reading and Spelling

Laura A. Robbins and Heather A. Kenny

Illustrated by Ken Stampnick

PORTAGE & MAIN PRESS

Portage & Main Press acknowledges the financial support of the Government of Canada through the Book Publishing Industry Development Program (BPIDP) for our publishing activities.

Printed and bound in Canada by Friesens.

Library and Archives Canada Cataloguing in Publication

Kenny, Heather A

A Sound approach : using phonemic awareness to teach reading and spelling / Heather A. Kenny and Laura A. Robbins.

Includes bibliographical references.

ISBN 978-1-55379-145-4

1. Reading—Phonetic method. 2. English language—Orthography and spelling—Study and teaching (Elementary). I. Robbins, Laura II. Title.

LB1573.3.K453 2007   372.46'5   C2007-906026-9

PORTAGE & MAIN PRESS

100-318 McDermot Ave.
Winnipeg, MB Canada R3A 0A2
Email: books@portageandmainpress.com
Tel: 204-987-3500
Toll-free: 1-800-667-9673
Fax-free: 1-866-734-8477

Printed on 30% PCW paper

Contents

Acknowledgments   ix

Introduction   1

Chapter 1: Phonemic Awareness, Decoding, and Encoding   9

Chapter 2: Phonological Awareness, Phonics, and Alphabetic Coding   19

Chapter 3: Activities for Large Groups, Small Groups, or Pairs   35
    Part 1: Ten Phonemic Awareness Activities   35
    Part 2: Six Decoding and Encoding Activites   44
    Reproducible Masters for the Activities   49

Chapter 4: Lesson Plans for Small Groups or Individuals   83
    Part 1: Seven Lessons for Teaching the Simple Sounds   88
    Part 2: Four Lessons for Teaching Consonant Digraphs   98
    Part 3: Six Lessons for Teaching Vowel Digraphs   101
    Reproducible Masters for the Lesson Plans   107

Appendixes
    Story Starters and Riddles   190
    Action Pages   203
    Visual Strips   229
    Pictures Pages and Words-and-Pictures Pages   231

Bibliography   257

For

Paul and Susan (L.R.)
Lauren, Claire, and especially Paul (H.K.)

Acknowledgments

We wish to thank the many students who have taught us about learning to read and spell, and the many dedicated educators, especially Penny Szpakowski, Wanda Bunt, Jane Mcgarvey, and Wilma Greenhalgh, who have so enthusiastically adopted the approach we present in this book and generously provided us with their feedback. We are particularly grateful to Linda DeGroot, who developed the tic-tac-toe word game that has become a favorite among our students.

Sincere thanks also go to Dr. Robert Allshouse and Dr. Patricia Pollifrone of Gannon University, and University of Toledo faculty members Dr. Eileen Carr and Dr. Jenny Denyer for providing professional guidance and much-needed personal support.

As always, we are most grateful for the love and support of our families and friends. Love and thanks go to: Paul and Susan Robbins, Paul, Lauren and Claire Kenny, Claire McCarthur, Palm Roberts, Robert and Marcia Allshouse, Ruth Kenny, Carol and Dan Farr, Diane Pezzini, Adele Roberts and Evan Guenkel, Lisa, Todd and Meghan Allshouse, Jo Ann, Mike, Jack and Luke Stanley, Margaret Lannon, Margaret Standen, Sharon McCaw, Dee Goodings, Ray and Tyler Wiese, and Sophie Taylor.

Aa Bb Cc Dd

Ee Ff Gg Hh

Ii Jj Kk Ll

Mm Nn Oo Pp

Qq Rr Ss Tt

Uu Vv Ww

Xx Yy Zz

Introduction

Arianna* sighed and gazed at her friends before turning her attention back to her teacher. The other children were happily engaged in a game of make-believe at the classroom house-center, which involved many props and a great deal of giggling. But Arianna sat, small and silent, at a table at one end of the classroom staring at the simple three-letter word before her. She knew what was expected of her, as this was by no means the first such session. Laura, who was her kindergarten teacher at the time, pointed to the word *bat*, printed in perfect ball-and-stick block letters, and said encouragingly, "Arianna, I want you to say each sound, then read the word." Arianna dutifully responded "/b/ - /a/ - /t/" as Laura pointed to each letter in turn. But, when Laura asked hopefully, "Now what word does that spell?" Arianna responded with her usual blank stare.**

After several more attempts, Laura tried a new tactic. "Okay, Arianna, look at the letters while *I* say the sounds: /b/ - /a/ - /t/. What does that spell? /b/ - /a/ - /t/." More blank stares. Undaunted, Laura switched gears yet again. "Arianna, *don't* look at the letter. Just look at me. Watch my mouth. What word am I saying? /b/ - /a/ - /t/. /B/ /aaaaaaaaaaaa/ /t/. Baaaaaaaaaaaat. What word am I saying?" Poor Arianna knew that she would not be able to play make-believe at the house-center until she responded correctly. "Box? Book?" she asked desperately, searching her teacher's eyes, as if to read the answer there.

The session ended, as did all the previous ones, when Laura finally took pity on Arianna for having sat so long and so patiently. "That's the word *bat*, Arianna. Let's read the word together: baaaaat." And with that, Arianna bounded off to the house-center, leaving Laura shaking her head in consternation. What puzzled her was that Arianna knew all 26 letters of the alphabet and the sounds most commonly represented by those letters. Why then, could she not sound out words?

---

*Some students' names have been changed.
** In this volume, phonemes are represented by common spelling patterns and are enclosed in slash marks.

That event took place almost a decade and a half ago. At that time, Laura was an experienced primary teacher and I had just recently graduated with my teaching degree. The high-needs urban elementary school where we taught was overcrowded and, while we each had our own kindergarten classes, we shared the same classroom. We believed then, as we do now, that the most important gift we could give our students was a strong foundation of literacy skills, and the majority of our efforts were directed at laying that foundation. Alongside many constructivist methods, we taught our students "old-school phonics." We taught them to identify the shapes and sounds of letters and then encouraged them to "sound out" unfamiliar words as needed. Armed with the ability to identify by sight a handful of frequently used words, most of our students were off to a good start, enthusiastically decoding simple texts. But we were puzzled and intrigued by students who, like Arianna, knew the names and sounds of the letters but could not sound out words.

Our initial solution was to give students like Arianna more instruction in phonics. Our rationale was simple: if they could not do it, then they must need more practice. We gave them practice in small groups with manipulatives; we gave them pen-to-paper activities; we coached them individually. Ironically, the students in our classes who could do the phonics activities were the ones who did not seem to need the practice, whereas the students who seemed to need the practice could not master the activities. No matter how many phonics activities we threw at them, students like Arianna simply could not sound out words. By the end of that year, we had given up on phonics instruction entirely for them and had adopted a strictly wholistic approach to reading. In our heart of hearts, however, we knew that we had failed them.

The following year, Arianna had moved on, but some of our new students were experiencing the same difficulties. We were determined to find a way to reach these students. We started by surveying the existing literature relating to reading instruction and came across a surprising number of studies that linked phonemic awareness to reading ability. At that time, few of our colleagues could not even pronounce the term, let alone define it. We decided that, if phonemic awareness was so important to reading acquisition, then we would learn enough about it to be able to teach our students.

Since that time, we have learned that decoding, or a child's ability to sound out words, is dependent on two factors. First, the child must have an understanding of how the alphabet works as a code for speech sounds. Arianna already knew that the letter *b* represented the sound /b/, the letter *a* represented the sound /a/, and so on. What was missing was the second piece of the puzzle: the child's phonemic awareness, that is, the ability to hear and manipulate the individual sounds, or phonemes, that comprise spoken words. Arianna's story is a cautionary tale. Had we understood the concept *phonemic awareness* and its significance to the acquisition of literacy skills, we would have provided Arianna with instruction targeted to develop her phonemic awareness and consequently her decoding skills. Arianna's problem was not that she could not learn through phonics but, rather, that her underdeveloped phonemic awareness prevented her from being able to access phonics as an effective reading strategy.

For the next decade, we continued to read and investigate phonemic awareness through the academic literature and through our own teaching practice. We worked collaboratively to develop and refine a phonemically driven approach to reading and spelling for both beginning and struggling readers. We began conducting professional-development seminars, first for teachers at local school boards, then at reading conferences across North America. Laura completed her master of education degree, specializing in literacy, and in her master's thesis she examined the phonemic awareness skills of kindergarten students. She took a position as a special-education teacher, conducting school-based action research that examined the effects of phonemic awareness instruction on the reading skills of struggling readers in grades one to eight. She is currently a literacy coach and resource teacher in Burlington, Ontario.

I resigned from my elementary-school teaching position and began working privately as an educational consultant, specializing in phonemic intervention and remediation. The students I tutored were identified with, or considered to be at-risk for, reading and/or spelling disabilities. I completed my master of education degree, specializing in literacy, and the focus of my master's thesis was on the intersection of professional development and teachers' knowledge of phonemic awareness. I am currently a full-time doctoral student and have taught literacy courses at the undergraduate and graduate levels at the University of Toledo.

This book is the result of our ongoing investigations. Since that time almost 15 years ago when we taught Arianna, we have developed and refined a phonemically driven approach to reading and spelling instruction. We have taught hundreds of beginning and struggling readers, aged five to 14 in large groups, in small groups, and individually, and we have had the kind of success that years ago we never would have dreamed possible. We have taught and learned from beginning readers; young students identified with reading and spelling problems, and other learning disabilities; and older students who, despite having undergone years of remedial instruction, still struggled with reading. With very few exceptions, our students have experienced great success. Laura now claims that, finally, after 30 years in the profession, she knows how to teach reading. Our goal in writing this book is to share what we have learned from other researchers and, just as important, what we have

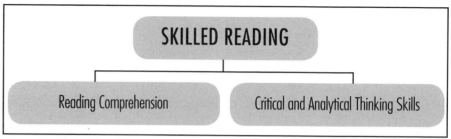

Figure I.1: Skilled Reading

learned from our own students. We know that, with the right approach, teaching children to decode and encode can be relatively simple, fun, and enormously rewarding for both students and teachers.

Throughout this book, we usually refer to reading in terms of *decoding*. But this is not to suggest that we consider the two words (*reading* and *decoding*) to be synonymous. Nothing could be further from the truth. *Decoding* refers to the process by which students are able to look at the arbitrary visual symbols that we call *letters* and translate them into spoken words. Colloquially, this process is referred to as *sounding out*. Reading, on the other hand, is an infinitely more complex cognitive process that carries implications far beyond the mere recitation of words on a page.

In order for students to be highly skilled as readers, they must be able to understand, interpret, and critically examine the message inherent in a text. However, like any other complex skill, reading can be broken down into requisite sub-skills. Let us examine reading from a top-down perspective. Please note that this discussion is not intended to be comprehensive or reflective of the considerable complexities of the overall reading process. Rather, it is intended to enable us to deconstruct and examine discrete elements of the process.

Let us begin by asking ourselves the following question: if our students are to become highly skilled readers, what knowledge and skills must they acquire? They must be able to (a) understand what they read and (b) apply critical and analytical thinking skills to texts. Skilled reading can therefore be broken down as shown in figure I.1.

Let us now turn our attention to the knowledge and skills that are required for students to be able to comprehend what they read. Reading comprehension implies three elements. First, students must be able to decode text fluently. Second, they must have well-developed background knowledge to be able to connect with the text as well as sufficient knowledge of the vocabulary that they will encounter. And, third, they must have well-developed comprehension skills. These elements are represented in figure I.2.

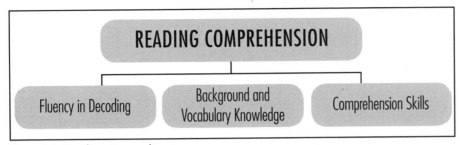

Figure I.2: Reading Comprehension

Now, let's examine the term *fluency in decoding* more closely. What are the knowledge and skills that students need to acquire in order to decode text fluently? As shown in figure I.3 (page 6), students need (a) a thorough knowledge of the alphabetic code and (b) well-developed phonemic awareness skills.

The model identified in figures I.1, I.2, and I.3 is highly simplistic and thus cannot possibly do justice to the complexity of the reading process. It does, however, demonstrate the importance of decoding skills to a child's acquisition of skilled reading. This is a top-down model, but if we are to teach our students the sub-skills necessary to be skilled readers, we need to approach reading instruction from the bottom up, for, if children lack phonemic awareness and alphabetic coding skills, they are necessarily unable to decode. If children are unable to decode, their comprehension skills are adversely affected; and, without the ability to comprehend what they read, students have no hope of becoming highly skilled readers.

We do not claim that this book represents a comprehensive reading program. We recognize that any good reading program incorporates effective instruction in all the elements discussed so far (critical and analytical thinking skills, activating background knowledge, vocabulary development, comprehension skills, fluency, decoding), as well as guided practice that teaches students to integrate them. Rather, in this book, we focus on decoding (reading) and its reciprocal skill, encoding (spelling). Our goal is to help you, the teacher, develop the knowledge and skills needed to effectively assess and teach phonemic awareness and alphabetic coding skills, thus enabling your students, in turn, to become skilled decoders and encoders.

In chapter 1, we investigate phonemic awareness and its link to reading and spelling (decoding and encoding). In chapter 2, we explore the relationship between phonemic awareness and the related terms *phonological awareness*, *phonics*, and *alphabetic coding*. In chapter 3, we introduce a variety of simple, classroom-developed activities that require few materials and minimal preparation. These activities will help your students master the phonemic skills of blending and segmenting, and will reinforce their

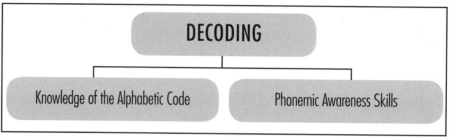

Figure I.3: Decoding

decoding and encoding skills in a manner that is fun and success-based. In chapter 4, we demonstrate in a series of lesson plans how to apply blending and segmenting to reading and spelling. The lesson plans follow a systematic, logically sequenced approach that links phonemic awareness to phonics and teaches beginning readers and struggling readers, alike, the fundamentals of decoding and encoding.

Chapters 3 and 4 and the appendix provide you with a host of resources and reproducible materials that will enable you to begin incorporating phonemic awareness and alphabetic coding instruction into your literacy program without delay. These materials include reproducible assessments, sound cards, word cards, and short-vowel cue cards, as well as action pages, pictures pages, words-and-pictures pages, and story starters and riddles.

Throughout chapters 3 and 4 we include sidebars, all entitled Research to Practise, which recount some of our classroom experiences as well as our interactions with other educators in the context of our professional-development workshops. These items are intended to respond to common questions and concerns, to give you a "feel" for this approach to reading and spelling instruction, and to generally help you to learn from our mistakes. We hope you find these sidebars both entertaining and enlightening.

If you are relatively new to teaching, or if you are new to teaching a phonemically driven approach to reading and spelling, you may wish to read the book from cover to cover. The same holds true if you are interested in an in-depth examination of the topics *phonemic awareness, phonological awareness, phonics, alphabetic coding, decoding,* and *encoding.* If, however, you are familiar with the rationale for this approach, you may simply wish to flip to chapters 3 and 4 and make use of the instructional strategies that we present. Feel free to copy the reproducible materials in the appendix as they are, or modify them to better suit your needs and the needs of your students.

Many of the lessons in chapter 4 are scripted for you. Our rationale for this is simple. First, we consider specific examples to be illustrations rather than mere instructions. Second, we believe it important that a certain type of language be used. This language is not always comfortable, nor does it come naturally at first. In our early days of using a phonemically driven approach, we would often find ourselves sitting in front of our students and feeling completely tongue-tied. After too many such experiences, we began scripting the lessons for ourselves, writing out little "cheat sheets" that we could refer to if we became stuck in the middle of a lesson. If you are already familiar with the language patterns we present in this book, you may wish to consider these scripts just as starting points or guidelines for your own lessons. If, on the other hand, you are like us in our younger days, you may choose to follow closely the scripts offered here.

It is our hope that you find the materials and activities included in this book easy to understand, fun, and easy to implement. Mastering phonemic awareness, decoding, and encoding skills is of vital importance to your students as they develop as readers and spellers. Our classroom experiences have demonstrated that the activities we present are inherently enjoyable for students and enormously rewarding for teachers.

Heather Kenny

Phonemic Awareness, Decoding, and Encoding

N o doubt you have heard the term *phonemic awareness* bandied about, but, like many teachers, you may not know exactly what it means or why it is crucial to students' success in learning to *decode* and *encode*. In this chapter, we define each of these terms, explore the relationships among them, and discuss their importance to children's overall literacy development.

PHONEMIC AWARENESS

Phonemic awareness can be defined as the ability to hear and manipulate the individual sounds in spoken language. It is the understanding that the word *dog*, for example, is made up of three distinct units of sound (/d/-/o/-/g/), and that it encompasses a child's the ability to blend sounds together to form spoken words and the ability to segment, or pull apart, the sounds within those words. For example, if we were to say the sounds /s/-/a/-/t/, you could blend them together to form the word *sat*. If we were to say the sounds /t/-/ee/-/ch/-/er/, you could blend them together to form the word *teacher*. You will notice that the spoken word *teacher* has only four sounds, even though the printed version of the word is spelled with six letters. Phonemic awareness is an auditory skill that relates only to the sounds in spoken words; it has nothing to do with the letters that appear in print. In order to appreciate the importance of phonemic awareness to overall reading and spelling development, you must first understand how spoken language is made up of phonemes and how phonemes can be orally blended, segmented, and manipulated.

Understanding Phonemes

The term *phonemic awareness* implies a child's consciousness of phonemes, the individual sounds that make up spoken language. Phonemes are the

Table 1.1: English-Language Phonemes

Consonants		Vowels	
/b/ (bat)	/s/ (sun)	/a/ (at)	/ow/ (how)
/d/ (dig)	/t/ (tan)	/e/ (get)	/er/ (flower)
/f/ (fit)	/v/ (vat)	/i/ (it)	/ar/ (far)
/g/ (girl)	/w/ (wish)	/o/ (odd)	/or/ (for)
/h/ (hello)	/y/ (yet)	/u/ (cup)	/oo/ (moon)
/j/ (jump)	/z/ (zeal)	/ai/ (rain)	/oo/ (look)
/k/ (king)	/sh/ (shop)	/ee/ (deep)	/oy/ (joy)
/l/ (lip)	/ch/ (chill)	/ie/ (pie)	
/m/ (must)	/th/ (thick)	/oe/ (coat)	
/n/ (net)	/th/ (then)	/ew/ (cue)	
/p/ (pin)	/zh/ (treasure)		
/r/ (run)	/ng/ (sing)		

(Ehri and Nunes 139; D. McGuinness xv.)

Note: qu and x each represent two phonemes (/k/-/w/ and /k/-/s/ respectively). Also note that we have not used the International Phonetic Alphabet to delineate these sounds. It has been our experience that most teachers are relatively unfamiliar with that system, and even many speech and language pathologists find its use cumbersome. Instead, we have chosen to represent the sounds with common spelling patterns. (The letter combinations *th* and *oo* are common spelling patterns that are used to represent two sounds: /th/ as in *thick*, and /th/ as in *then*; /oo/ as in *moon* and /oo/ as in *look*.) Throughout the book we have provided key words so as to eliminate any ambiguity.

smallest distinguishable units of speech—the fundamental building blocks of a language. While the precise number of phonemes in English varies according to dialect, there are approximately 41 sounds in the English language (see table 1.1). Every word that we speak is made up of one or more phonemes. Most words are made up of a combination of sounds, although a few words, such as the word *I* and the word *a,* consist of only one phoneme.

Although they are small units of sound and the differences between them are frequently subtle, phonemes wield tremendous linguistic power. It is just a single phoneme that can change a *fish* to a *wish*, a *pet* to a *pot*, and a *snip* to a *sniff*. Children learn to speak by attending to and producing the sounds that they hear. Very quickly, however, their attention to phonemes gives way to the imitation of words. When children begin to produce words, the phonemes overlap and become virtually indistinguishable as individual units of sound. The great irony is that, when they start learning to read, children must turn their attention back to the individual sounds in words, sounds that have no meaning in and of themselves. According to Marilyn Adams in *Beginning to Read: Thinking and Learning about Print,* "regaining conscious awareness of the phonemic structure of speech is among the most difficult and critical steps toward becoming a reader" (412).

Blending and Segmenting Phonemes

Blending is the phonemic sub-skill that is directly linked to decoding, whereas segmenting, the reciprocal skill, is directly linked to spelling. This statement may seem rather abstract, so let us give you some concrete examples to help clarify these concepts. Imagine the following scenario: a kindergarten teacher is seated in front of a blank chalkboard. Her students are gathered at her feet. The teacher is looking into the faces of the children, who, in turn, are watching her mouth closely.

Teacher	I'm going to say the sounds in a word, and I want you to tell me what the word is: /c/-/a/-/t/. (As she articulates the sounds in the word, the teacher leaves a one-second interval after each sound.)
Students	cat
Teacher	Very good. Let's try a more difficult word: /f/-/l/-/ow/-/er/ (Once again, the teacher leaves a one-second interval after each of the sounds.)
Students	flower
Teacher	Excellent!

These students have just demonstrated their ability to blend phonemes; they have taken individual sounds and blended them together to form spoken words. You will notice that the teacher did not write either the word cat or the word flower on the chalkboard. This was strictly an oral language activity. The only visual cue to which the students had access was their teacher's mouth as she carefully articulated the sounds. You will also notice that the teacher recognized that the word flower was slightly more difficult to blend than the word cat; as the number of phonemes in a word increases, so does the level of difficulty in blending or segmenting them. But these students were up to the challenge. They were able to take discrete sounds and blend them together to form both cat and flower. Blending is the phonemic sub-skill that is directly linked to a child's decoding, or reading, ability.

The teacher continues:

Teacher	Now I'm going to say a word, and I want you to tell me each of the sounds in that word. The word is *sit.* (The teacher holds up her left hand in a fist and extends her thumb.)

Students	/s/ (The teacher extends her index finger, leaving her thumb extended.)
Students	/i/ (The teacher extends her middle finger, holding up all three digits.)
Students	/t/
Teacher	What word did you say? (The teacher pinches all three extended fingers together.)
Students	sit
Teacher	Terrific! Let's try another word: *clap*. (The teacher holds up the same fist and extends her thumb, index, middle, and ring fingers in turn as her students say each corresponding sound.)
Students	/c/-/l/-/a/-/p/
Teacher	What word did you say? (The teacher pinches her fingers together.)
Students	clap
Teacher	Excellent!

This time, the students were engaged in segmenting words. They took seamless spoken words and pulled them apart into distinct, individual phonemes. You will notice that the teacher's use of her thumb and fingers to cue the students was deliberate and served several purposes. First, by using her left hand, she reinforced the directionality of print. From the students' perspective, her fingers moved in a left-to-right direction, each finger representing a single sound. This action mimics how children learn to decode text: letter by letter in a left-to-right fashion. Second, by cueing them with her fingers, she ensured that her students left a one-second interval between each sound, thus effectively segmenting the word, rather than just stretching it out. Finally, by first extending and then pinching her fingers together, she represented the way sounds can be articulated individually and then blended together to form a single, spoken word. The second task (clap) was slightly more challenging than the first (sit), as adjacent consonants (often referred to as *consonant blends*) are among the most difficult sounds in the English language to segment.

Phonemic blending and segmenting are reciprocal skills; however, of the two, segmenting is the more difficult task. In order to segment, students must take a spoken word, pull it apart into individual phonemes, and leave an auditory space between each of the sounds, indicating where one sound ends and the next begins. (Printed words have visual spaces between them, and so readers are able to tell where one word ends and the next begins.) Segmenting is highly unnatural, given the seamless nature of spoken language. When we speak, we do not leave auditory spaces between words, let alone between individual sounds within words. And, to further complicate things, some phonemes are difficult to pronounce in isolation.

Take, for example, the sound /b/. /B/ is what speech and language pathologists refer to as a "stop" sound. In isolation, it should be pronounced only as a "pop." It cannot be elongated; to do so, you would have to "vowelize" it by attaching the sound *uh* to the end of the consonant, which distorts the sound. If the sound /b/ were vowelized, for example, it would be pronounced *buh*. Vowelizing is a practice that can be particularly problematic for struggling readers. Let us visit a different kindergarten classroom. In this scenario, the teacher is standing in front of the chalkboard on which is printed, in perfect ball-and-stick letters, the word *cap*. The students are seated facing the chalkboard, looking up at the word.

Teacher	Let's sound out this word. (The teacher points to the letter *c*.) What sound does the letter *c* make?
Students	kuh (The teacher then points to the letter *a*.)
Students	/a/ (The teacher points to the letter *p*.)
Students	puh
Teacher	What word does that spell?

Several students immediately shout out *cap*, while others in the class are left to stare at the word in puzzlement. Arianna is one such student. She has no idea what she is supposed to do when her teacher asks the students to sound out a word. Arianna lacks the ability to blend and segment phonemes. Although some students in the class have developed blending and segmenting skills spontaneously (without any special instruction) Arianna has not. She cannot sound out anything.

Anwar is inherently phonemically aware, but, when he tries to blend kuh-/a/-puh (the vowelized "sounds" that his teacher has taught him), all he can come up with is *kuapuh*, not *cap*. Not surprisingly, *kuh-/a/-puh* sounds markedly different from the sounds /k/-/a/-/p/, which comprise the word *cap*. Like Arianna, Anwar struggles with decoding, but for a different reason. A child's success in decoding depends on two factors: a knowledge of the sounds that letter-symbols represent and the ability to blend those sounds in order to recognize the spoken form of the word. Arianna cannot blend sounds, and hence she cannot decode. Anwar has a distorted concept of the sounds /k/ and /p/ (both of which should be pronounced as stop sounds).

Consequently, he, too, is unable to recognize the spoken form of the word *cap*. Neither Arianna nor Anwar can sound out words effectively, and this is a problem that is likely to have lasting and detrimental effects on their decoding, and hence their reading, abilities (see McGuinness).

Vowelizing is not the only problem demonstrated in this second scenario. The teacher has asked, "What sound does the letter *c* make?" Although such a question is hardly unusual in primary classrooms across North America, it is misguided and potentially misleading to students. If, for example, the letter *t* makes the sound /t/, then why is the sound /t/ not in the words *the* or *thin*? The answer is simply that *t* does not make the sound /t/. *T* does not *make* anything. The letter *t* is merely a visual symbol that is used to represent the sound /t/ in the word *cat*. This distinction is subtle, but it is crucial to understanding how the letters of our alphabet are used as a code for speech sounds. Although the visual symbol *t* can be used to represent the sound /t/ (as in the word *talk*), it can also be used in combination with the letter *h* to represent the sound /th/ as in *thin*, or the sound /th/ as in *then*. Individual letters (such as the letter *t*) and combinations of letters (such as the letters *t* and *h*) are merely visual representations of the spoken sounds of our language (see McGuinness).

Manipulating Phonemes

Blending and segmenting are by no means the only tasks associated with phonemes. Manipulating phonemes is another. It involves either deleting or substituting a phoneme or phonemes. Let us give you some examples. This time we are going to ask you to play along as if you were a student. Try deleting a sound within a word. Say the word *sun*. Now say it again without the /s/. The answer is, of course, *un*. Try another example: say the word *nest*, then and say it again without the /s/. That task was a bit more challenging, wasn't it? You had to separate the adjacent consonants /s/ and /t/ in order to delete the sound /s/ and form the word *net*. Many struggling readers are able to segment simple consonant-vowel-consonant (CVC) words but are unable to break apart adjacent consonants.

Substituting phonemes is an even more challenging task. Try changing the /o/ in the word *stop* to /e/. The new word is *step*. Now change the /a/ in the word *cat* to /oe/. If you substituted the sound /a/ for the sound /oe/, you should have come up with the word *coat*. But, if you responded with *cot*, you are by no means alone. Many teachers at the workshops we give respond by saying *cot*, probably because, as adults and as skilled readers, we are not used to attending to individual sounds in words. Rather, we pay close attention to spelling patterns. Had we asked you to change the letter *a* to the letter *o*, *cot* would have been the correct answer. Instead, we asked you to substitute sounds.

This exercise highlights the fundamental difference between phonemic awareness and phonics. Phonemic awareness is an auditory skill. It is not at all related to letters or to print. Phonics, on the other hand, links sounds to spelling patterns. If you changed the word *cat* to *cot*, you were engaged in mental phonics. You were imagining the spelling of the word *cat*, you removed the letter *a*, substituted the letter *o*, and "read" the word as *cot*.

DECODING AND ENCODING

The term *decoding* can be defined as the ability to translate written symbols (letters) into spoken words. For example, if we were to show you the letters *j u m p*, you would be able to translate them into the spoken word *jump*. The term *encoding* is, quite simply, the reverse of decoding. It is one's ability to translate spoken words into written symbols. If we were to say the word *plant*, you would be able to record the corresponding letters *p l a n t*.

You will notice that we make reference to the "spoken" forms of words. Skilled readers do not necessarily recite words out loud as they read, but they nevertheless do translate sequences of letters into the spoken forms of the words they are reading. Try reading the following passage without engaging in a running commentary in your head. Do not allow yourself to "think" the spoken words as you read them.

> Readers normally acquire strategies for active comprehension informally. Comprehension strategies are specific procedures that guide students to become aware of how well they are comprehending as they attempt to read and write. (National Institute of Child Health and Human Development, 40)

If you were successful in preventing yourself from thinking the spoken forms of the words (a difficult, if not impossible, feat), chances are that you were unable to understand and follow the message in the passage. That is because, in order to retrieve meaning from strings of letters, we must first connect them to spoken words (see Adams), if only in our "mind's ear." Thus, when we read, we "hear" the words on the page, even if we are not reading aloud.

It is important to note that decoding and encoding are not synonymous with reading and writing. Reading and writing are far more complex skills, which involve a host of higher-order cognitive processes. Decoding and encoding are, by comparison, lower-order skills. That being said, we must stress that decoding is a necessary precursor to skilled reading (see pages 4 and 5). If children cannot quickly and accurately decode words, then they will be unable to focus on comprehending the message of a text. Students with especially poor decoding skills may be unable to even access the message of a text. Children who struggle with encoding often have so much difficulty spelling that they cannot convey their messages effectively through writing, and these children often find writing a difficult and onerous task.

If phonemic awareness is an auditory skill that has nothing to do with written language, why then is it so crucial that we learn to decode and encode? Pretend for a moment that you are a student. We are going to say the sounds in a word, and we want you to tell us what the word is: /g/-/l/-/a/-/d/. Did you say *glad*? Congratulations, you are phonemically aware! You can blend sounds together to form a spoken word. But what does that have to do with reading ability? Pretend now that you have never seen the following word:

w e n t

We want you to say each sound individually and then blend the sounds together to read the word. Think for a moment about what you just did. If you had not been able to blend those sounds together orally, would you have been able to sound out that word? Of course not. In order to successfully decode, or sound out, words, you must be able to recognize the sounds that the letters represent (for example: the letter *w* = the sound /w/; the letter *e* = the sound /e/; and so on) and blend the sounds together orally to form the spoken word.

Let us look at a different example. Try reading the following word:

You cannot read it at present because you do not have the requisite knowledge. You have no way of knowing which sounds these arbitrary symbols are intended to represent. So, the first thing you must do is learn the sound-symbol correspondences (phonics).

♦ = /t/   )(= /i/   □ = /p/

Now are you able to read that word? How about this word?

And this word?

Before you learned the sound-symbol correspondences, you were unable to successfully decode this written language because you lacked sufficient *knowledge* about what these arbitrary symbols were intended to represent. Nevertheless, chances are that you already possessed the *skills* you needed in order to decode. Once you gained the requisite knowledge, you were able to decode the words *tip, it,* and *pit.* This lesson in phonics was successful, but only because you were *already* phonemically aware.

Students like Arianna, who lack the ability to blend sounds, are consequently unable to decode words. No amount of phonics knowledge will help them sound out words effectively if they lack the phonemic skills required to decode. We have interviewed many struggling readers in grade 3 and above who, when asked to sound out words, had no idea what to do. These students could not understand what the term *sound out* meant because they could not blend sounds. Phonemic awareness is therefore the step before phonics. In order for children to be able use their knowledge about letters and sounds and to decode words, *they must first be phonemically aware.*

As you can see, a student's ability to blend is crucial to his or her ability to decode. It would stand to reason, then, that a student's ability to segment (the reciprocal skill) would be crucial to his or her ability to encode (spell). Such is the case. If you were a child who wanted to spell an unfamiliar word, what knowledge and skills would you need in order to be successful? Pretend once again that you are a student and that you wanted to spell the following word:

r e s t

The first thing you would need to do is segment the sounds in that word: /r/-/e/-/s/-/t/ (phonemic awareness). Then you would need to know how those sounds are represented by letters (phonics): the sound /r/ is represented by the letter *r*; the sound /e/ is represented by the letter *e*; and so on. Your knowledge of the sound-symbol correspondences enabled you to record the sounds that you heard in that word. But you would not have known which sounds to record if you had not been able to segment them first.

Once we, the authors, recognized the importance of phonemic awareness to reading and spelling, we began to incorporate blending and segmenting instruction into our literacy program. We were surprised and delighted to find that our students were fascinated by this new way of manipulating spoken language. It was not uncommon for us to witness scenarios much like this:

> Lauren and Justin were seated at the craft center amidst a sea of multi-colored construction paper. Pencils, crayons, and markers were scattered about the table. Both students were deeply involved in their own projects. Justin looked up and noticed a pair of scissors in Lauren's hand. "Hey, Lauren! Give me your /sc/-/i/-/ss/-/or/-/s/," he commanded. Lauren glanced up at him briefly before turning her attention back to her creation. Without missing a beat, she responded, "Get your /ow/-/n/."

Parents also reported random acts of blending and segmenting. One father told me with a chuckle that, whenever he teased his daughter, she would "sound him out." "/D/-/a/-/d/!" she would exclaim, "/s/-/t/-/o/-/p/ it. Right /n/-/ow/!"

As interesting as it was to see how the children were able to transfer their blending and segmenting skills to contexts outside of school, what was most thrilling for us was the manner in which they were able to transfer those skills to the context that mattered most: reading and spelling. Phonemic awareness has no intrinsic worth. Its value lies only in its capacity to help children understand and access the alphabetic code to read and write effectively. But as Adams observes, "the extent [to which] children do have [phonemic awareness] skills, reading instruction can be fruitful and to the extent that they do not, it cannot" (56–57).

2

Phonological Awareness, Phonics, and Alphabetic Coding

By now, you probably have a good general understanding of the terms *phonemic awareness*, *decoding*, and *encoding*, and you understand their importance to a child's literacy development. There is an additional set of terms, however, that are related—*phonological awareness*, *phonics*, and *alphabetic coding*—and these are often confused with *phonemic awareness*, *decoding*, and *encoding*. It is important that we distinguish among these concepts. In this chapter, we examine each of the three new concepts in turn and discuss how they differ from *phonemic awareness*, *decoding*, and *encoding*, as well as their implications for literacy instruction.

PHONOLOGICAL AWARENESS

Like *phonemic awareness*, *phonological awareness* refers to the sounds in spoken language and has nothing whatsoever to do with printed language. Yet, while *phonemic awareness* refers specifically to a sensitivity to phonemes (the smallest unit of sound), *phonological awareness* refers to "a sensitivity to *any size unit of sound*" (Yopp and Yopp 131, emph. in original). Thus, the term *phonological awareness* is an umbrella term that encompasses a number of skills of varying degrees of difficulty (including phonemic awareness). Table 2.1 shows various phonological tasks on a continuum from simple to complex. As the table shows, the recognition of rhyming patterns and recitation of nursery rhymes are relatively simple phonological tasks, which children typically master in their preschool years. For example: sat, cat, hat, bat, mat; Humpty Dumpty sat on a *wall*. Humpty Dumpty had a great *fall*. Another relatively simple phonological task shown in table 2.1 is segmenting a sentence into individual words. For example: Humpty – Dumpty – sat – on – a – wall. A slightly more complex task is breaking a single, multi-syllabic word into syllables. For example: hel – i – cop – ter; di – no – saur.

Table 2.1: Phonological Skills Continuum

Recognizing rhyming patterns or nursery rhymes	Segmenting sentences into individual words	Blending and segmenting syllables	Blending and segmenting onset-rime components	Blending and segmenting phonemes

→ →

Simple	More Complex	Most Complex

The next step along the phonological continuum is further subdividing a single syllable (either a single-syllable word or a single syllable within a multi-syllabic word) into onset and rime components. *Onset* refers to any consonant or group of consonants that comes before the vowel. *Rime* refers to the vowel plus whatever comes after it. The rime is the part of the word that rhymes. Consider the examples in table 2.2.

The last step on the Phonological Skills Continuum is phonemic awareness: the most complex of all of the phonological tasks, and it is the only skill that is directly linked to decoding (reading) and encoding (spelling). The great irony in this is that the phonological skills required for reading develop in reverse order to the order in which children draw upon those skills in their reading development (see table 2.3 on page 22).

Among the very first skills that beginning readers need to master is that of decoding words. Yet this most basic, fundamental reading skill is dependent on phonemic awareness, the most complex phonological skill, and the one that is typically the last of all the phonological skills to develop.

Once children have had sufficient practice in decoding and encoding simple words, they begin to recognize common spelling patterns (also referred to as *orthographic patterns*). Instead of having to sound out /a/ and /t/ to decode words such as *at, sat,* or *mat,* at this stage they begin to recognize the sound chunk *at,* and they draw upon their onset-rime blending skills to read these words automatically. Finally, as they begin to encounter longer, multi-syllabic words, children draw upon their ability to blend syllables in order to read these words.

Another great irony is that the most important of all the phonological skills (phonemic awareness) is often the most neglected. In preschool and kindergarten, children are typically engaged in a host of rhyming games and activities. They practice chants and learn to segment sentences into words; they play games in which they blend and segment syllables. By the end of kindergarten or the beginning of first grade, children are often given practice blending and segmenting onset-rime components. They are introduced to

A Sound Approach

Table 2.2: Subdividing Single-Syllable Words

Word	Onset	Rime
split	spl	it
spit	sp	it
sit	s	it
it	–	it

consonant blends such as *br, cr, dr, fr, gr,* and so on, and they blend those sound units with rimes (often referred to as word families) such as *at, it, in,* and *an.* Yet the phonological instruction often ends there. Many children never receive direct instruction in the phonological skills that will have the most direct and positive effect on their reading and spelling abilities: the blending and segmenting of individual phonemes. The lessons, games, and activities included in this book are designed to help you assess and teach your beginning and struggling readers these crucial reading sub-skills.

PHONICS

If you are not entirely sure about the difference between *phonemic awareness* and *phonics,* you are by no means alone. It is the question most frequently asked by teachers at our workshops. Even in professional resources, the two terms are often used interchangeably.

Phonemic awareness refers to blending and segmenting the individual sounds in spoken words. The term *phonics* refers to a method of reading instruction that emphasizes sound-symbol correspondences. Rudimentary phonics instruction teaches children that the letter *a* spells the sound /a/, the letter *b* the sound /b/, and so on. Once children learn these basic sound-symbol correspondences, phonics instruction teaches them to sound out, or decode, simple words. Children sounding out the word *sat* would look at each letter individually, say the corresponding sounds (/s/-/a/-/t/), then blend the sounds together to read the word. Blending sounds is a necessary step in the process. If children lack the ability to blend sounds orally, they are simply unable to decode words. And without the ability to decode words, they cannot benefit from phonics instruction.

The difference between phonemic awareness and phonics can be summed up in a single word: letters. As soon as we attach visual symbols (letters) to sounds, the activity is no longer phonemic awareness; it is phonics. Look back at our first scenario in chapter 1 (pages 11 and 12): the teacher was sitting in front of a blank chalkboard looking into the faces of her students. The children, in turn, were watching her mouth closely as she

Table 2.3: Reading Skills and Requisite Phonological Skills

Reading Skill	Phonological Skill Required
Decoding simple words	Phonemic Awareness
Fluency in recognizing simple orthographic (spelling) patterns	Onset-rime blending
Decoding multi-syllabic words	Syllable blending

directed them to blend and segment words. These students were engaged in a phonemic awareness activity; they were not attending to the letters in the word; they were focusing exclusively on the sounds. The only visual cue to which they had access was their teacher's mouth.

The teacher in the second scenario in chapter 1 (page 13) was standing in front of a chalkboard on which was printed the word *cap*. Her students were seated in front of her, looking up at the word. She instructed them to say each sound aloud, then read the word. These students were engaged in phonics.

Phonics is an important—even essential—part of any learn-to-read program. With a strong foundation of phonics skills, children are able to decode unfamiliar words—words that they may have never seen before. When this happens—as it should—reading becomes a self-teaching mechanism (see Adams). But, without the ability to decode, students have limited options for identifying an unknown word. They could (1) ask somebody to tell them the word (this strategy is likely to soon become very tiresome), (2) memorize the word, or (3) predict the word based on other cues. None of these options is effective as a primary reading strategy, the first for obvious reasons, and the latter two for more subtle, yet equally compelling, reasons.

Let us examine memorization as a primary reading strategy. When learning to read, children must rely, to some degree, on visual memory. They need to memorize the shapes of letters and other visual symbols, such as punctuation marks. In addition, they need to memorize in their entirety a finite number of words. Beginning readers frequently rely on visual patterns to memorize words such as *mom, dad, dog, cat,* and so on. While this strategy can be effective in the short term, memorizing every new word that comes along is not a good long-term option (see Adams). There are simply too many new words to learn.

There is a natural limit to the capacity of the human brain to memorize arbitrary visual symbols such as letters, numbers, and whole words. Even students with outstanding visual memories can never hope to memorize every word they encounter in print (McGuinness 50), since there are between

1.2 and 2 million words in the English lexicon, with an additional 1 200 to 20 000 new words added each year (Rasinski et al.).

Students who over-rely on visual memory to identify words can appear to be very successful readers in the early primary grades. But, as their reading vocabularies expand, their visual memories become overloaded, and they begin to experience more and more difficulty acquiring new words and distinguishing among familiar words. Take, for example, the words *house* and *horse*. These words are commonly misread by children who over-rely on visual memory. Without the benefit of picture cues, it is easy for these students to mistake *house* for *horse* or *horse* for *house*. With the exception of one medial letter, the two words are identical. Yet students who have good decoding and word-analysis skills do not tend to make such mistakes. They intuitively recognize that the letters *ou* could never spell the sound /or/, nor could the letters *or* ever spell the sound /ow/ (see McGuinness).

Now let us examine prediction as a primary reading strategy. In the early primary grades, children can be quite successful in predicting words using their knowledge of initial sounds and context cues. If a sentence in a picture book reads "The man rode his h____," there is usually a big picture of a horse to go along with it. In this context, children at the early primary level can predict most words with relative ease. The students did not actually analyze the word; they just made an educated guess based on picture cues. And, while they will probably be able to guess correctly most of the time throughout their early primary years, they will not be able to rely on this strategy to serve them when the words start getting bigger and the accompanying pictures start getting smaller. The problem lies in the fact that context cues are largely unreliable: "The child depends on the meaning of the passage to infer the meaning of its less familiar words, yet the meaning of the passage depends disproportionately on the meanings of its less frequent words" (Adams 217).

Try a decoding exercise that we frequently use in our workshops. The exercise is scheduled just before a coffee break; we ask teachers to complete it on their own and not to share their answers with anyone until after the break. Decode the following message, using the key shown in table 2.4. Fill in your answer in the blanks, or, if you really want a challenge, try doing it mentally:

___ ___ ___   ___ ___   ___   ___ ___ ___ ___ ___

Almost all our workshop participants are able to successfully decode the first three words (Time for a …), although, admittedly, some have difficulty with the word *a*; they are surprised that the word *a* is composed of the same phoneme as the vowel sound in the word *cup*. It is the fourth word that generally causes difficulty. We typically find that teachers fall into one of

Table 2.4: Alphabetic Symbols Key

♌	= /b/ as in *bat*	♠	= /ee/ as in *see*
●	= /f/ as in *fan*	⌘	= /ie/ as in *pie*
□	= /m/ as in *man*	◆	= /u/ as in *cup*
❖	= /n/ as in *new*	○	= /ow/ as in *cow*
■	= /r/ as in *red*	⌘	= /or/ as in *store*
◆	= /t/ as in *top*		

two camps: those who rely on their decoding skills to analyze and correctly identify the word as *brownie*; and those who use initial consonant and contextual cues to predict (incorrectly) the word as *break*. So, what happens when you look only at the first few sounds and predict the word based on context cues? You miss the brownie!

Our decoding exercise also demonstrates how mentally challenging it can be to decode words on a letter-by-letter, sound-by-sound basis. You might ask why, if our ultimate goal is to enable our students to recognize entire words quickly and effortlessly, we subject them to the letter-by-letter sounding-out strategy that is so laborious for them (and so painful for us to witness). Would it not be more efficient to teach students to recognize words wholistically? In short, no! We know that letter-by-letter decoding is a necessary precursor to proficient reading (see Moats, *Teaching*). And, without spending the requisite time learning how letters are used to represent sounds and how those sounds combine to form words, children cannot develop the word-analysis skills required for skilled reading.

We must also bear in mind that the early stages of any complex skill bear little resemblance to the later, more developed, stages. Let us use a concrete example to illustrate this phenomenon. Playing hockey is a complex skill that is composed of a number of sub-skills, including skating, stopping, and puck-handling, to name just a few. Highly skilled hockey players, like those in the National Hockey League (NHL), are fluent in all the necessary sub-skills, and they are able to easily and seamlessly integrate those skills. If you have ever watched an NHL game, you will know that such highly skilled players can make skating and puck-handling look natural, even graceful.

Now let us imagine that we are watching a group of four- and five-year-olds playing hockey. Instead of gliding gracefully across the ice, passing the puck effortlessly from one player to the next, these children move haltingly, occasionally stumbling and sprawling face-first onto the ice. The puck is rarely passed from one player to the next. When it is, it typically lands far from any of the skaters, and the spectators must wait patiently while the tiny players make their slow and laborious trek to retrieve it.

The game played by four- and five-year-olds looks very different from an NHL game, yet we know that every player in the NHL was once a five-year-old. Those players ended up as professionals not because they found a way to avoid skating or stopping or puck handling but because they practiced until they developed fluency in each of the requisite sub-skills.

Like playing hockey, reading is a complex skill. Highly skilled readers make reading appear natural and effortless, but this impression belies the many hours that they have spent mastering and learning to integrate the sub-skills required for fluent decoding. Many educators erroneously assume that the goal of phonics instruction is merely to teach children to decode words. In fact, however, phonics instruction is intended to enable students to identify words so effortlessly that their conscious attention can be devoted solely to the comprehension of text (see Adams).

Now let us turn our attention back to our decoding exercise. If you correctly decoded the word *brownie*, then you did exactly what skilled readers do. Skilled readers typically analyze and process every letter of every word that they come across (McConkie and Zola, as cited in Adams 101). We do not mean to imply that when reading, skilled readers do not make use of contextual prompts, including semantic (meaning) and syntactic (grammar) cues. These cueing systems are used frequently, but they are used most effectively to confirm rather than to identify the meanings of words. Let us give you an example of the type of scenario that we witnessed countless times when working with our beginning and struggling readers:

> Santiago, a delightful kindergarten student with a rich, melodic voice, is reading aloud the following sentence: "The man was kind to his dog." Initially, he sounds out the word *kind* using the short vowel sound /i/. This behavior is natural, since he has been taught the sound-symbol correspondences for the short vowels. But Santiago knows that the words he reads are supposed to sound like spoken words. He immediately recognizes that this pronunciation does not sound like a word and, without prompting, he examines the rest of the words in the sentence, determines the correct pronunciation of the word *kind*, and rereads the sentence correctly.

Santiago was developing the habits of a good reader. The written word *kind* was unfamiliar to him, but, rather than looking at the first sound and guessing at the word, he attempted to decode it in its entirety. His preliminary decoding efforts did not result in the correct pronunciation of the word, but it did provide him with what we term a *phonetic approximation*. The phonetic approximation sounded enough like the actual word that, when he combined this information with contextual cues, he was able to correctly identify the word. We were of, course, not privy to Santiago's thought process, but, if we had been, then we may have heard something like the following. (Santiago's spoken words are enclosed in quotation marks. His thoughts are enclosed in square brackets.)

> "The – man – was – /k/-/i/-/n/-/d/…" [K/i/nd? No, that can't be right.]

> "The man was k/i/nd – to – his – dog." [I wonder if it's the word *kind*. That would make sense. (Santiago examines the word *kind* more closely.) Yeah, that word looks like it could spell *kind* /k/-/ie/-/n/-/d/, kind.]

> "The man was *kind* to his dog!"

Heather recalls another example of the effective use of a phonetic approximation combined with contextual cues to correctly determine the meaning of a word. She was in her second year of high school when she first encountered the word *epitome* in print. When she initially attempted the word, she pronounced it as *e-pi-tome* (with the emphasis on the first syllable and the final syllable rhyming with the word *comb*). She immediately recognized this pronunciation as a non-word and used the context to determine that it must be *e-pi-to-me* (with the emphasis on the second syllable). Heather distinctly remembers the sudden flash of understanding when she realized, "Oh! So that's how you spell *epitome*!" Both Heather and Santiago, thanks to their decoding skills, were able to use reading as a self-teaching activity.

Compare Santiago's and Heather's reading behaviors with Connor's. Connor was a struggling reader in third grade when his parents sought the help of a private tutor. As part of an initial series of assessments, the tutor asked Connor to read a passage from an appropriate grade-level text. It quickly became apparent to the tutor that Connor, while bright and articulate, had poor word-identification skills. Whenever he came across an unfamiliar word in the text, he used the initial consonant or consonants to guess at the word. The problem was that his guesses, while reasonable, were often incorrect. Once, after spending several minutes reading about a "strange mouse" and desperately trying to make sense of the passage, Connor gave up. As it turned out, the mouse was not so strange after all. In fact, there had never been a mouse; the passage was about "strong magic."

Students like Connor, who are unable to analyze words, often must rely on guessing (or prediction) to identify unknown words. When used as a primary word-identification strategy, predicting is highly inefficient and often has dire consequences.* For example: Anthony, at the tender age of

---

*Although making predictions is ineffective as a primary word-identification strategy, it is highly effective as a comprehension strategy. Students should be encouraged to make predictions in order to better understand texts.

eight, had given up on expecting his reading to make sense. Consequently, he did not bother to pay attention to whether the words he read were real words or nonsense words. This behavior—which initially seems very strange—is disturbingly widespread amongst students who struggle with decoding. Anthony's tutor reported that, whenever he came to an unfamiliar word, Anthony's voice would drop, and he would mutter something unintelligible, then carry on reading. If his tutor asked him to stop and reread the section of text a bit louder, Anthony's reading would sound a bit like this: "The schmuh…was trub in the fluv."

Stephanie, a fifth grader, at least recited real words. Unfortunately, those words often made no sense when strung together. If a text read "They went to the store to buy apples and bananas," Stephanie's reading would sound something like this: "They went at the stair to but apple a bandana." When the resource teacher heard Stephanie's oral reading, the teacher asked, "Stephanie, why are you reading that way? Your reading doesn't make any sense." Stephanie thought for a moment and then replied, "Well, most of the time I read to myself. No one can hear what's in my head, so when I make mistakes it doesn't matter. I can just keep going."

ALPHABETIC CODING

Phonemic awareness instruction is important, but it is not sufficient to ensure that learners will be able to decode and encode successfully. Children must also understand how letters represent sounds. This understanding is referred to as a knowledge of the alphabetic code, which is not to be confused with the alphabet. The *alphabet*, a term used to describe the 26 symbols from *A* to *Z*, is merely a set of letters that are used to spell words. The term *alphabetic code* refers to the correspondence between the sounds in words and the letters or letter combinations that are used to spell those sounds.

Recall for a moment our phonics lesson in chapter 1 (page 16). We asked you to read the following word:

Initially you could not read it because you did not have the requisite knowledge. You did not know which sounds those arbitrary symbols were intended to represent. Once you learned the representations (you gained alphabetic-code knowledge), you were able to successfully read the word as *tip*. The same is true, of course, for children: before they can successfully decode and encode, they must have sufficient knowledge of the alphabetic code.

Note that we used the qualifier *sufficient* in reference to students' knowledge of alphabetic coding. We taught you individual sounds that were represented by individual symbols. This system of representation—one sound as represented by one letter—is referred to as a "one-to-one" mapping pattern, and it is the simplest mapping pattern in English. But, unfortunately, it is not the only mapping pattern.

As noted in table 1.1 (page 10), there are approximately 41 English sounds but only 26 letters. Some sounds must therefore be represented by combinations of letters. Hence, the letters *s* and *h*, which represent the sounds /s/ and /h/ individually, are combined to spell the sound /sh/. Such letter combinations are referred to as *digraphs*.

Digraphs are not to be confused with *consonant blends*, a term commonly applied to adjacent consonants. For example, the letters *ch* in the word *chip*, make up a digraph. When we segment *chip*, we break it down into the phonemes /ch/ - /i/ - /p/. The letters *c* and *h* work together to spell a single phoneme: /ch/. Contrast this with the consonant blend *gr* in the word *grip*. When we segment *grip*, we break it down into the phonemes /g/ - /r/ - /i/ - /p/. The letters *g* and *r* are each used to represent a different phoneme (the *g* represents /g/; the r represents /r/). These phonemes can then be blended together to form the sound unit *gr*, hence the term *consonant blend*.

Most beginning and struggling readers are familiar with simple one-to-one mapping patterns. Kindergarten students typically are taught the letters of the alphabet and the sounds that those letters most commonly represent. Primary students are also taught the most common consonant digraphs. Even many struggling readers know that the letters *ch* represents the sound /ch/, the letters *sh* the sound /sh/, and the letters *th* the sounds /th/ (as in *thin*) or /th/ (as in *then*), and they can identify the initial sound or sounds within words.

What beginning and struggling readers and spellers are often unfamiliar with are vowel digraphs such as *ou*, *au*, *igh*, and (our personal favorites) *eigh*, *aigh*, *oul*, and *ough*. These complex letter combinations are rarely taught as acceptable spelling patterns for the sounds that they represent, and, consequently, children are often at a loss about how to analyze words that contain them. To complicate matters further, students rarely receive direct instruction about what to do with the letters after the initial consonants. Since children are often taught to over-rely on sight-word knowledge or prediction skills, they frequently get into the habit of taking a close look at the first few letters and a quick glance at the word ending, and then largely ignoring whatever is in the middle. Over time, the overuse of these strategies promotes sloppy reading.

We have heard countless well-meaning teachers lament that they cannot understand why their struggling readers do not pay close attention to words. The teachers' rationale is that, if their students would only look more carefully at each word (that is, sound it out), then word identification, and hence reading skills, would improve. While there is some truth to this logic (that is, that struggling readers have often been taught to rely so heavily on memorization and initial consonants that they do not bother attending to the medial and final parts of words), it is important to acknowledge that the problem is often far more deeply rooted. Even if these children were taught to look carefully at words in their entirety, chances are that they still would not know what to do with them. Even with well-developed phonemic blending and segmenting skills (which an overwhelming percentage of struggling decoders do not possess), it is likely that these struggling students would still lack sufficient knowledge about the complex elements of the alphabetic code.

Inasmuch as English is a complex, irregular language, be heartened: there are far more regularities than there are irregularities. Even words that are typically considered to be irregular are usually more regular than they are irregular. Take, for example, the word *friend*, which is often treated as a sight word because of its irregular spelling pattern. First, let us segment it into phonemes: /f/ - /r/ - /e/ - /n/ - /d/. Now let us match the spelling patterns to the sounds in the word: f = /f/; r = /r/; /ei = /e/; n = /n/; d = /d/. Four of the five sounds in the word *friend* are represented by simple, one-to-one mapping patterns. Hence the word is 80 percent regular and only 20 percent irregular. Only the sound /e/ is represented by an uncommon spelling pattern.

Let us now pretend that we are beginning readers who are familiar with only one-to-one mapping and a few frequently used sight words, such as *my, play, with, me,* and *is.* We are given a simple story to read. The text reads as follows: "My dog Sam plays with me. He is my best friend." We are able to identify the word *my* based on our sight-word knowledge. *Dog* and *Sam* are highly decodable words. And we are able to read the remainder of the first sentence and the beginning of the second based on our knowledge of sight words. We are left, then, with the words *best* (which we can decode) and *friend*.

We might use initial consonants to predict (guess) the word *friend*. But, if we started with a phonetic approximation instead, we would begin by sounding out the word as follows: /f/ /r/ /i/ /e/ /n/ /d/. When we read the entire sentence, we get: "My dog Sam plays with me. He is my best fri-end." Provided that we have been monitoring our reading and that we have the word *friend* in our speaking vocabulary, we would automatically self-correct and read the word correctly. Our phonetic approximation (fri-end), combined with an understanding of the context of the sentence, is sufficient to enable us to recognize the word as *friend*.

Table 2.5: Recommended Sequence of Instruction for Blending, Segmenting, Decoding, and Encoding

Grade Level	End-of-Year Objectives	Page Numbers
K	✓ Students will recognize and be able to record the most common sounds associated with the 26 letters of the alphabet.	Lesson 1.1 (90–93)
	✓ Students will be able to auditorally discriminate between all short vowel sounds, using kinesthetic mnemonic cues as needed.*	Activity 2.3 (45–46) Lesson 1.1 (90–93)
	✓ Students will be able to blend, segment*, read and spell two and three phoneme words (VC and CVC) that employ one-to-one mapping patterns.	Activity 2.4 (46–47) Lesson 1.2 (93–94) Lesson 1.3 (94–95) Lesson 1.4 (95–96) Lesson 1.5 (96)
	✓ With guidance, students will begin to use decoding skills to identify unknown words in context.*	Lesson 1.7 (97–98)
	✓ Students will begin to use encoding skills to phonetically spell words in their own writing.	Lesson 1.6 (97)
1	✓ Students will demonstrate mastery of all of the skills developed in the previous year.	
	✓ Students will be able to discriminate auditorally between short vowel sounds rapidly and with automaticity.*	Activity 2.3 (45–46)
	✓ Students will recognize and be able to record the following digraphs: sh, ch, th, ck, er, ir, or, ur, ar.*	Lesson 2.1 (99) Lesson 3.1 (101–103)
	✓ Students will recognize and be able to record three common spelling patterns for each of the long vowel sounds.*	Lesson 3.1 (101–103)
	✓ Students will be able to blend, segment, read and spell single syllable words (including CCVC, CCGVC, CVCC, CVCC, CCVCC words)* using all familiar mapping patterns (including digraphs)*.	Lesson 2.1 (99) Lesson 2.2 (99–100)
	✓ Students will independently decode simple words in the context of a story.	Lesson 2.4 (101)
	✓ Students will use knowledge of digraphs to phonetically spell words in their own writing.	Lesson 2.3 (100)
2	✓ Students will demonstrate mastery of all of the skills developed in previous years.	
	✓ Students will recognize and be able to record common spelling patterns for all phonemes.*	Lesson 3.1 (101–103)
	✓ Students will be able to blend, segment, decode and encode words containing familiar spelling patterns.*	Lesson 3.2 (103–104) Lesson 3.3 (104–105) Lesson 3.4 (105)
	✓ Students will use decoding as a primary word identification strategy (phonetic approximations) and use meaning and grammar cues to confirm the meaning of unknown words when reading independently.*	Lesson 3.6 (106)
	✓ Students will use knowledge of common spelling patterns to approximate conventional spelling in their own writing.*	Lesson 3.5 (105–106)

Note: Although they are not represented on this table, many older readers who are struggling—those beyond second grade—will also need direct, targeted instruction in phonemic awareness, alphabetic coding, decoding, and encoding skills. For these students, we strongly recommend that you assess their knowledge and skill level prior to planning instructional interventions. (Reproducible Phonemic Awareness and Alphabetic Coding assessments can be found on pages 107 to 115.)

*These are crucial skills that are frquently under-developed in struggling readers.

Now let us look at another possible phonetic approximation. Let us say that we recognized the digraph *ie* and know that it can spell the sound /ie/. We sound out the word, but, this time, we come up with: /f/ /r/ /ie/ /n/ /d/. Our pronunciation will be wrong (frynd), but, once again, the approximation is close enough to *friend* to enable us to recognize the word in context.

Rather than relying on prediction strategies (which, if over-used in the long run, will ultimately undermine our reading attempts) in the exercise that we just did, we used our decoding skills to analyze the word on a sound-by-sound basis, and reading was a self-teaching activity. We were able to identify a previously unknown word (*friend*), and we would have a very good chance of recognizing it, or at least of being able to decode it again if we encountered it in another section of text. The beauty of this system (that is, using decoding as a primary word identification strategy, then confirming the meaning of the word by using contextual cues) is that, in addition to promoting strong decoding skills, it promotes comprehension. Students must monitor their own reading and constantly ask themselves, "Is that a word I know? Does that word make sense?"

Had Anthony (page 26) been taught this strategy (and the phonemic awareness and alphabetic coding sub-skills required to employ this strategy), his oral reading would not have included non-words such as *schmuh, trub,* and *fluv*. Had Stephanie (page 27) learned to monitor for comprehension at the word level, she would not have been content to read a nonsensical sentence such as "They went at the stair to but apple a bandana."

We are often asked by school- and district-level administrators what a sequence of instruction in the primary grades should look like. Their basic questions are usually What should be taught and when? and How do we ensure that students are taught everything that they need to know in order to be successful decoders and encoders? Table 2.5 outlines a recommended sequence of instruction and links the objectives to the sections of the book that include strategy instruction in those skills.

A WORD ABOUT SIGHT WORDS

Every letter of every word in the English language is used to spell, or to help spell, a sound in a word. In that sense, any English word could potentially be decoded. All one would need to know is how those letters (or spelling patterns) represent sounds. However, given that English is an irregular language that has been subject to a wide variety of influences, including other languages (see McGuinness), some accepted spelling patterns are so rare, or appear to be so illogical, that it would be absurd to teach them as patterns at all. Instead, it makes sense to introduce students to those words discretely, and to encourage them to recognize these words in their entirety. We refer to

After introducing kinesthetic cues for various sight words, Laura noticed that several of her second-grade students who were struggling with sight-word identification would act out the actions associated with these words while reading stories silently or in small groups. When reading aloud with Laura, if a child could not recall the sight word, Laura would silently demonstrate the action associated with the word. This cue would immediately help the student identify the word. When these words became part of the students' working memory, they no longer need to rely on the actions.

such words as *sight words*. Just as children memorize the arbitrary symbols that we call letters, so too can they memorize a limited number of seemingly arbitrary letter sequences.

In our own teaching, we classify words into three categories: highly decodable words, semi-decodable words, and sight words. Highly decodable words are, simply, those words that contain common spelling patterns and that can be decoded easily. Words such as *mom, dad, dog,* and *cat* fall into this category, as do words such as *cake, book,* and *snore* (provided that students have learned the accompanying spelling patterns). Strong decoders are able to recognize such words based on their spelling patterns alone. They do not need context to aid them in word identification.

We use the term *semi-decodable* to refer to words that are decodable within the context of a story. We consider the word *his* to be one such word. If a child were reading the text "Sam and his dog went home," the child might initially pronounce the word *his* as *hiss*. This pronunciation would be quite normal, since the student has probably been taught that the letter *s* typically spells the sound /s/. *Hiss* is a phonetic approximation that is relatively close to the actual pronunciation of the word *hiss*. When presented with meaning and grammar cues embedded in the context of the sentence, the child can easily self-correct and accurately identify the word.

Sight words are highly irregular in their spelling patterns. Unfortunately for beginning readers, it is often the shorter, higher-frequency words that tend to fall into this category. Such words cannot be reliably identified even with contextual cues. For your reference, we include a chart listing words that we believe should be taught to students by sight (see table 2.6). Please note that there may be other words that could be included in this chart. We recommend, however, that, before choosing to teach any word by sight, you give careful consideration to the distinction among highly decodable words, semi-decodable words, and sight words. Remember that decoding is a high-yield strategy. Armed with a knowledge of the alphabetic code and the ability to blend the sounds in words, children can identify hundreds of words in isolation, and thousands more in the context of their reading experiences. Conversely, to teach a word by sight is to add but a single word to a child's reading vocabulary.

You will notice that some of the sight words on our list can be decoded (*for, like, see,* just to name a few). The problem is that these words are so common that they are frequently encountered by beginning readers, who are just being introduced to the simplest, most basic elements of the alphabetic code (one-to-one mapping patterns) and have no knowledge of digraphs. We recommend that you teach these words only as needed, adding them to a sight word-wall as you introduce them. We also recommend that you

Table 2.6: Sight Words

again	green	orange	today
always	he	out	two
are	her	please	use
because	here	purple	very
blue	I	said	was
brown	like	saw	we
by	look	say	were
come	love	see	what
do	made	so	when
down	make	some	where
eight	me	that	white
five	my	the	who
for	nine	then	why
four	no	there	you
gave	now	this	your
go	once	three	
good	one	to	

incorporate kinesthetic mnemonic cues for words that students struggle with. In the same way that we recommend actions for each of the simple sounds (see the action pages in the appendix, starting on page 203), we suggest that kinesthetic cues can be equally effective for teaching basic sight words. For example, you might teach students to point to themselves for the word *me*, point to a friend for the word *you*, or use a calling-towards-you action for the word *come*.

You might wish to involve your students in creating personalized, meaningful cues for various sight words. Remember that the action is intended to be a kinesthetic cueing system: the very act of pointing to themselves helps students recall the word *me*. Although, in this example, the action is linked to the meaning of the word, it is not necessary to attempt to match an action to the word's meaning. For example, one group of students chose to tap their wrists whenever they came across the word *the*. The action was not linked to the meaning of the word (the word *the* has no tangible meaning), but the mnemonic was effective nonetheless.

English is by no means a simple language to learn to read or spell. However, with proper instruction, students can successfully navigate the complexities of the alphabetic code to become expert decoders and encoders, and, consequently, enthusiastic readers.

Activities for Large Groups, Small Groups, or Pairs

Phonemic awareness, decoding skills, and encoding skills are crucial to a student's overall literacy development. But, just because they are crucial does not mean that they have to be taught through boring, drill-type exercises. In fact, quite the opposite is true. Our experiences have demonstrated that learning these skills can be fun and engaging for students. In this chapter, we include a variety of easy and effective activities designed to develop or reinforce your students' phonemic awareness, decoding skills, and encoding skills. Some of the activities are auditory and do not include any reference to letter symbols. Others rely on letter symbols to help children make the jump from phonemic awareness to phonics.

PART 1: TEN PHONEMIC AWARENESS ACTIVITIES

Activity 1.1: Sounding Out Attendance

One of the easiest and most effective ways we have found to incorporate phonemic awareness instruction into our program on a regular basis is by sounding out the daily attendance. We recommend that you make a special class list for this activity, in which all the students' names are spelled phonetically. This activity can be used with large or small groups.

Materials

- class attendance list (for teacher reference only); find a reproducible master for an attendance list on pages 49 and 50

Instructions

Say each sound in a student's name. Invite the entire group to call out the name and ask the student whose name is called to raise a hand. As students become more proficient, ask them to listen for the sounds in their own names, and have each individual call out his or her name. For example:

Teacher	I am going to say the sounds in someone's name. /P/ -/au/ -/l/. Whose name is it?
Students	Paul (Paul raises his hand.)

Continue with remaining names. Do this activity several days a week, or even daily, throughout the entire first term.

At the beginning of the academic year, there will likely be several students in your class who struggle with this activity. That is why, for the first few weeks, we recommend that you invite the entire class to call out the names rather than put individual students on the spot. It will become quickly apparent which children can hear the sounds of their names and which children have to rely on the responses of their classmates to cue them. After several weeks of sounding out attendance regularly, have only the student whose name is being called respond. There still may be some students who need extra support, and you can cue them by looking them directly in the eye and saying, "Are you ready? Your name is coming up next!"

Variations

The variations listed here are intended to teach phonemic awareness directly. Students need time to learn, practice, and consolidate each new skill in order to achieve mastery, therefore we recommend that you spend a minimum of three weeks on one activity before introducing the next. The variations are listed in approximate order of difficulty—from simple to more complex—so we also recommend that you do the activities in the order presented. We strongly recommend that, before you engage in any activity that changes students' names, you request permission to use their names in a silly way.

Variation 1: Omit the first sound in each student's name. For example:

Teacher	I am going to say a name that is missing the first sound. Whose name is it? Auren.
Students	Lauren

Variation 2: Omit the last sound in each student's name. For example:

Teacher	I am going to say a name that is missing the last sound. What is the last sound in the name Paul? Pau…?
Students:	/l/

Variation 3: Change the first sound of each student's name to a familiar sound. For example:

Teacher	I am going to change the first sound in someone's name to /p/. Pusan. Whose name is it?
Students	Susan

Variation 4: Instruct students to provide the final sound in each name. For example:

> **Teacher** I'm going to say a name and I want you to tell me the last sound in that name. Catherine.
>
> **Students** /n/

Variation 5: Segment and count the sounds in each name. For example:

> **Teacher** I'm going to say a name, and I want you to say each of the sounds with me. I am going to count the sounds on my fingers. Ready? The name is Tyler.
>
> **Teacher and Students** /T/ /ie/ /l/ /er/ (The teacher extends one finger to represent each sound, then pinches her fingers back together.) Tyler
>
> **Teacher** How many sounds does Tyler have in his name? (The teacher extends four fingers up to cue the students.)
>
> **Students** four

An extension of this variation might be to invite students to graph the number of sounds in their names.

Variation 6: Instruct students to change the first sound in their names. Our experience has demonstrated that, while most children enjoy such activities, a few find it embarrassing. We substitute another variation for those students who prefer not have their names changed.

For example:

> **Teacher** My first name is Heather. If I changed the first sound to /w/, my name would be Weather. What would your name be if you changed the first sound to /w/? Todd?
>
> **Todd** Wodd

You can modify this activity as needed for students whose names begin with vowel sounds or adjacent consonants. For example, a child such as Arturo, whose name begins with a vowel, would not be able to substitute a /w/ for the first phoneme in his name; it would not be phonetically legitimate. Instead, he could add the sound /w/ to the beginning of his name. Similarly, a child with a name like Claire would not be able to substitute /w/ for the first sound in her name. She could, however, substitute the /w/ for the adjacent consonants *c* and *l*. Thus, Claire would become Waire.

Variation 7: Instruct students to count the sounds and provide the final sound in each name. For example:

RESEARCH TO PRACTICE

Often the spellings of names can be deceptive. A number of years ago, Heather had a student named Rachel in her kindergarten class. While Rachel never caused any trouble in the classroom, her name caused Heather a month's worth of grief. At the beginning of the school year, when she first started using taking attendance as in variation 6, Heather would sound out her name as follows: /r/-/ae/-/ch/-/e/-/l/. She knew that wasn't quite right, and could tell by the faces of her students that it didn't sound right to them either. Finally, after of month of frustration, Heather marched down the hall to Laura's classroom and demanded that she segment the name *Rachel*. Laura responded, "/r/-/ae/-/ch/-/l/". "What about the *e*?" Heather asked. "What about the *e*?" was Laura's response. "The e and the l spell the sound /l/." Without even realizing it, Heather had been trying to impose a sound on the letter e, when, in fact, e didn't "make" a sound. It was used in combination with l, to spell the sound /l/. After "The Rachel Inciden,t" we both made a conscious effort not to think about how the name was *spelled* but, rather, to focus on the sounds that we heard.

| Teacher | I am going to count all the sounds in someone's name except for the last one. I want you to tell me the last sound. Ready? Diane. /D/-/i/-/a/…(The teacher extends one finger for each sound as she says them and then holds up a fourth finger, indicating that the students are to respond.) |
| Students | /n/ |

Variation 8: Have students provide the last two sounds in each name. For example:

Teacher	I'm going to say the first few sounds in a name and, when I hold up my fingers, I want you to tell me the last two sounds. Watch my fingers. Ready? Lisa: /L/-/ee/…(The teacher extends one finger, indicating that the students are to respond.)
Students	/s/ (The teacher extends a second finger, indicating that the students are to respond.)
Students	/a/

Activity 1.2: Blending Categories

Blending categories is a game that is very effective for students who are just learning to blend and for students who are struggling with the concept of blending. This activity can be used with large groups, small groups, or pairs.

Materials

- a list of categorized words; you may select a category of words based on a theme or a random category from the list on pages 51 and 52, or simply make up a list of your own

Instructions

Identify a category of words for your students and invite them to blend a word within that category. For example:

| Teacher | I'm going to say the sounds in the names of some animals. I want you to tell me the animals. The first one is /d/-/o-/g/. What animal it is? |
| Students | dog |

Continue with other words in the same category.

Extensions

Extension 1: Challenge students to think of words in a given category. Invite them to take turns segmenting the words and "being the teacher."

Extension 2: Ask students to act out or demonstrate a category of actions or emotions. For example, say, "Show me your /h/-/a/-/p/-/p/-/y/ face."

Activity 1.3: Segmenting Categories

Segmenting is more difficult than blending, so it is best not to introduce your students to segmenting until they have experienced success at blending phonemes. Since segmenting can be challenging for some students, be sure to keep modeling both the word and the segmented form of the word until they are able to do it independently. This activity may be used with large groups, small groups, or pairs.

Materials

- a list of categorized words that contain between three and five phonemes (for teacher reference only); you may select a category of words based on a theme or a random category from the lists on pages 51 and 52, or simply make up a list of your own

Instructions

Identify a category of words for your students and invite them to segment a word within that category. For example:

Teacher	I'm going to say each sound in a color word. The word is *red*. The sounds in the word *red* are /r/-/e/-/d/. (The teacher allows a one-second interval between each sound. She counts the sounds on her fingers as she says them aloud.) What word did I just say?
Students	red (The teacher pinches her fingers together to visually cue the students.)
Teacher	Now, say each sound in the word *red*.
Students	/r/-/e/-/d/ (The teacher encourages her students to count the sounds on their fingers as they say the sounds aloud, then blend the sounds back together.) red

Continue with other words in the same category.

Extensions

Extension 1: As your students become proficient, you may choose not to model the answer. For example, simply ask, "Who can tell us the sounds in a color word?"

Extension 2: Ask your students to act out an emotion (happy, sad, excited, surprised, angry). For example, "Say the sounds in the word *happy* with a happy face." Or, "Say the sounds in the word *sad* with a sad face."

RESEARCH TO PRACTICE

Heather has been blending and segmenting with her daughter Claire since Claire could speak. Claire's name, however, was problematic. Heather knew that, in theory, *aire* is not a single phoneme, but whenever she tried to break it down, it just did not sound right. So Heather treated *aire* as a sound chunk, segmenting her daughter's name as /C/-/l/-aire rather than attempting to break up the final chunk and risk distorting the pronunciation. The same held true for several of our kindergarten and primary students who had the sound chunk *aire* in their names (Mary, Karen, Aaron). We firmly believe that, in the rare instances when you come across a sound chunk that just does not sound right when broken down, it is more important to be true to the pronunciation of the name than to break it down "correctly" and risk distorting it. The irony of this tale is that, despite "incorrect" modeling from her mother, once Claire was able to segment her name independently, she segmented it into the four "correct" phonemes.

Activity 1.4: First/Last Sounds

The first/last sounds game is effective for the handful of students who consistently leave off the first or last sound when they are trying to blend. (For example, after listening to the sounds /s/-/a/-/t/, such a student may respond *at*.) This activity may be used with small groups or pairs.

Materials

- a list of three- and four-phoneme words that begin with the same sound or end with the same sound (for teacher reference only); use one of the lists provided on page 53, or simply make up a list of your own

Instructions

Tell your students that all the words that you will be segmenting begin (or end) with the same sound. Emphasize the target sound by saying it louder than the other sounds. For example:

Teacher	I'm going to say sounds in some words that all begin with /sss/. Let's practice saying the sound /sss/.
Students	/sss/
Teacher	Can you tell me what this word is? /sss/ /a/ /t/
Students	sat

Continue with other words that begin (or end) with the same sound

Activity 1.5: I Spy

I spy is a fun and easy game for reinforcing students' blending skills. It is a variation on the traditional game of I spy in which an object is described with clues such as colors or shapes. Here, the individual sounds in the word identifying the object are the clues. This game is perfect for transitional times (while waiting in line for the bus, just before the bell rings, for example) and can be used for large groups, small groups, or pairs.

Instructions

Pick out an object in the room and segment the word identifying it. For example:

Teacher	I spy a /d/-/e/-/s/-/k/. What is it?
Students	desk

Continue with other objects in the room.

Extensions

Extension 1: Invite individual students to "spy" and segment the word that identifies something in the room. Or play a rhyming I-spy game. For example, say to the students, "I spy something in the room that rhymes with *besk*." Students would respond with *desk*.

Extension 2: Use a poster or story book and invite students to "spy" and segment something in the picture.

Activity 1.6: Simon Sounds

The Simon-sounds game is always a huge hit with our students. Like the game of I spy, Simon sounds is perfect for times when you have just a few minutes to fill but want to keep your students engaged. This game may be used with large groups, small groups, or pairs.

Instructions

Simon sounds is a variation of the game Simon says. Instruct your students to do a variety of tasks or exercises by sounding them out. For example, tell your students, "Do ten jumping /j/-/a/-/ck/-/s/."

Extension

Invite individual students to play the part of Simon and sound out the instructions.

Activity 1.7: Round-Robin Rhyming

The game of round-robin rhyming helps students learn to substitute initial sounds and recognize word families. Before beginning, it is important that you model the question and answer so that your students have a good understanding of the expectations and can be successful. This game may be used with large groups, small groups, or pairs.

Materials

- a list of rhyming words that contain three phonemes (for teacher use only); use one of the lists provided on page 54, or simply make a list of your own

Instructions

Have your students sit in a circle and give each student a turn to create a rhyming word. For example:

Teacher   We're going to play a rhyming game. The first word rhymes with *at*. Say *at*.

Students	at
Teacher	I'm thinking of a word that rhymes with *at* and begins with the sound /s/. What is my word?
Students	sat
Teacher	(The teacher turns to the first student.) I'm thinking of a word that rhymes with *sat* and begins with the sound /c/. What is my word?
First Student	cat
Teacher	(The teacher turns to the second student.) I'm thinking of a word that rhymes with *cat* and begins with /h/. What is my word?
Second Student	hat

Continue until every child in the group has had a turn.

Extensions

Extension 1: Without giving the initial sound, challenge students to think of the rhyming word. For example, "Can you think of a word that rhymes with *sat*?"

Extension 2: Invite students to play the role of teacher.

Extension 3: Increase the level of difficulty by rhyming with four- or five-phoneme words.

Activity 1.8: Following Directions by Blending

Following directions by blending is a fun and easy game that helps students improve their listening skills and their blending skills. It can be used with large groups, small groups, or pairs.

Instructions

As teachers, we often give our students directions to follow. Instead of simply telling students what to do, try selecting several words to segment into individual sounds. For example:

Teacher	I would like everyone to sit down at their /d/-/e/-/s /-/k/. (The teacher pauses to allow students time to sit down at their desks.) Now take out a piece of /p/-/a/-/p/-/er/.

Extension

Incorporate the following-directions-by-blending game into other curriculum areas, such as art, physical education, or math.

Activity 1.9: Storytelling by Blending Words

Story time is an important part of the daily school routine, as it provides an excellent opportunity for you to show students how their blending skills can be put into practice in the context of classroom reading experiences. When you are reading to your students, engage them in a storytelling-by-blending-words game. Simply segment one of the words in the story and ask the students to blend the word. We recommend that you start with simple three-, four-, and five-phoneme words—and invite your students to say the word. But do not overdo it. A few words are more than enough. You want your students to be able to enjoy and appreciate the flow of the story. Use the storytelling-by-blending-words game with large groups, small groups, or pairs.

Materials

- a story book

Instructions

When reading a story to your students, segment a few words from the story into their individual sounds. Pause to allow the students to blend the sounds and say the word. For example:

Teacher	Once upon a /t/-/ie/-/m/ (The teacher pauses and looks at the students.)
Students	time
Teacher	in a far away /l/-/a/-/n/-/d/
Students	land

Activity 1.10: Silly Songs and Rhymes

We recommend that you ask students' permission before using their names for silly songs and rhymes. Use silly songs and rhymes with large groups, small groups, or pairs.

Materials

- chart paper
- dry-erase marker

Instructions

Sing a familiar song or recite a familiar rhyme by substituting a familiar sound for the initial sounds of the words in the song or poem. For example, sing "Happy Birthday," replacing all the initial sounds in the song with the

---

RESEARCH TO PRACTICE

When Laura first used the story-telling-by-blending game in a kindergarten class, her students were very enthusiastic about it. They loved to chime in with the blended forms of the words. Laura was so encouraged by their response, however, that she over-did it. She began segmenting two or three words on every page. One day, Laura overheard a little voice in the back whispering in dread, "Oh no, she's going to do that for the rest of the story!" Laura learned her lesson well. Now she limits the number of words segmented to three or four at the very beginning of the story.

RESEARCH TO PRACTICE

Primary students love singing silly songs or chanting silly rhymes. We found that, initially, students find the activity quite challenging, but they typically experience success because they are so highly motivated. Eventually, we did link phonemic awareness to phonics by writing the songs on chart paper so that our students could follow along.

---

sound /s/ ("Sappy Sirthday soo sou. Sappy Sirthday soo sou…" Write a few of these songs on chart paper, leaving out the initial consonants or leaving a space in front of a word that begins with a vowel. The chart can be laminated so that you or your students can change the initial sound with a dry-erase marker.

PART 2: SIX DECODING AND ENCODING ACTIVITIES

Activity 2.1: Sound Concentration

Use sound concentration with small groups or pairs.

Materials

- two identical sets of sound cards for the simple sounds; initially, select five sounds (10 cards in total) that have been previously taught; as you teach more sounds, add them to the activity; find reproducible masters for sound cards for the simple sounds on pages 55 to 59

Instructions

Prepare playing cards by cutting out the individual sound cards and laminating them. Mix up the cards and lay them face down. The first player flips over one card, says the sound, then selects another card to flip over. If the sound represented on the second card is different from the first, the child says the sound aloud and then replaces both cards, face down. If the cards match, the player picks up the two cards. Play continues until all the cards have been matched.

Extensions

You can make sound cards with capital letters or alternate spellings by using the reproducible blank sound cards found on page 61.

Extension 1: Mix upper- and lower-case letters on the sound cards. For example, if a student turns over a lower-case letter *a*, that student must match it with an upper-case letter *A*.

Extension 2: Include alternate spellings on sound cards. For example, include the letters *c*, *k*, *ck*, and *cc* on individual sound cards. Since all these spellings are used to represent the sound /k/, a match can be made by using any two of those cards.

Activity 2.2: Go Fishing for Sounds

Use the go-fishing-for-sounds activity with small groups or pairs.

Materials

- two sets of sound cards for the simple sounds; initially, select five sounds (10 cards in total) that have been previously taught; as you teach more sounds, add them to the game; find reproducible masters for sound cards for the simple sounds on pages 55 to 59

Instructions

Prepare playing cards by cutting out and laminating the individual sounds. Deal three to five cards to each player. Place the remaining cards face down in a go-fish pile. The first player takes a turn by asking another player for a sound that matches one of their cards. For example, if Jamal had the letter *t*, he might say, "Lauren, do you have the sound /t/?" If Lauren has the letter *t*, she passes it to Jamal, who makes a match by laying down the matching cards. If Lauren does not have a match, she tells Jamal, "Go fish." Jamal then draws a sound card from the go-fish pile. The next player then gets a turn. Play continues until one or all of the players have matched all of their cards.

Extensions

You can make sound cards with capital letters or alternate spellings by using the reproducible blank sound cards found on page 61.

Extension 1: Mix upper- and lower-case letters on the sound cards. When a student asks for the sound /a/, the other student can provide an upper- or a lower-case letter *a*.

Extension 2: Provide sound cards with familiar alternate spellings. For example, provide sound cards with the letters *c*, *k*, and *ck*. If a player has a *c* and asks for the sound /k/, a *c*, *k*, or *ck* could be used to make a match.

Extension 3: Instead of making matches, invite students to form words. For example, if a student has the sound cards /s/ and /u/, the student might ask for /n/ to form the word *sun*.

Activity 2.3: What's in the Middle?

Use the what's-in-the-middle activity with large groups, small groups, or pairs.

Materials

- a short-vowel cue card (each one contains all five vowels) for each student; find reproducible masters for short-vowel cue cards on page 60

Instructions

Use a short-vowel cue card to review the short vowel sounds. Tell the students, "I'm going to say a sound. I want you to repeat the sound after me and, with your finger, trace the letter that spells that sound: /a/." Repeat this activity with the remaining short-vowel sounds on the short-vowel cue card.

Instruct the students: "I'm going to say a word, and I want you to listen for the sound in the middle. Then I want you to say that sound and trace the letter that spells it. The first word is *pat*." Students respond with /a/ and trace the letter *a*. Continue with other one-syllable words that contain short-vowel sounds, such as: *puck, pack, peck; spin, spun, span; pet, pit, pot, pat, putt; fan, fun, fin*. Repeat this lesson as needed, until students are able to distinguish short vowel sounds quickly and accurately.

Modification

If the what's-in-the-middle activity is too difficult for some students, modify it as follows: After reviewing the short-vowel sounds, tell the students, "I'm going to say a word, and I want you to listen for the sound at the beginning. Then I want you to say that sound and trace the letter that spells it. The first word is *at*." Students respond with /a/ and touch the letter *a*. Continue with other two-phoneme words containing short vowel sounds. (Try using nonsense words such as *ag, et, ip, og*, and *uf* in addition to real words.)

Extensions

Extension 1: Once students become adept at recognizing the short-vowel sounds in consonant-vowel-consonant (CVC) words, increase the level of difficulty by challenging them with CCVC, CCVCC, CVCC, or CCCVCC words.

Extension 2: Divide your class into groups of two to four students. Provide each group with a set of word cards for simple sounds (pages 62 to 81) and a short-vowel cue card (page 60). Instruct your students to take turns reading a word from a card, asking the other students to trace the letter on the cue card, then saying the sound.

Activity 2.4: Building Words

Use the building-words activity with small groups or pairs.

Materials

- make sound cards for each sound in three simple, decodable three-phoneme words; print the sounds in each word in the same color, for example: *s, u,* and *n* in yellow; *n, e,* and *t* in red; *t, i,* and *p* in blue; find reproducible blank sound cards on page 61; laminate the cards

- a small, zip-sealed plastic bag

RESEARCH TO PRACTICE

Short vowel sounds are the most difficult sounds in the English language for children to distinguish. Many at-risk readers have great difficulty distinguishing between the sounds /i/ and /e/, or the sounds /o/ and /u/. We have had great success with this activity with both beginning and struggling readers. For beginning students, we would start by targeting only two or three vowel sounds (for example, /a/, /i/ and /o/). As the other short vowel sounds are formally introduced, we would begin to include them in the game. With struggling readers we would target only the sounds that they had trouble with (usually either /i/ and /e/ or /o/ and /u/). After a few weeks of practice with this game, we noticed a marked improvement in their ability to segment and correctly discriminate between the short vowel sounds.

Instructions

Place all the sound cards in the plastic bag. Have students open the bag, sort the sound cards by color, build a word with each group of cards, then read the words. (For the letter combination *n*, *e*, and *t*, either the word *net* or *ten* would be acceptable.)

Variation

Have students build nonsense words and read them out loud.

Activity 2.5: Beat the Clock

Use the beat-the-clock activity with small groups or pairs.

Materials

- word cards for the simple sounds for previously taught sounds; find reproducible masters for word cards for the simple sounds on pages 62 to 81

- a stopwatch or a watch or clock with a second hand

Instructions

Prepare playing cards by cutting out the individual sounds and laminating the cards. Make a pile. Tell your students that they need to read as many words as possible in one minute. Select the top card and have the first student read the word. Select the second card and have the second student read the word. Continue with the other students in the group until the time is up. Count the number of cards read by the group. If time allows, challenge the students to read even more words within the same time period.

Extension

Once students have begun to master decoding as a primary strategy, include non-decodable (sight) words in the word pile. (For a discussion of sight words, see chapter 2, page 30.)

Activity 2.6: Tic-Tac-Toe

Have your students play tic-tac-toe in pairs.

Materials

- word cards for the simple sounds for previously taught sounds; find reproducible masters for word cards for the simple sounds on pages 62 to 81

- a tic-tac-toe game board; find a reproducible tic-tac-toe game board on page 82

Instructions

Prepare playing cards by cutting out word cards and laminating them. Make a pile. The first player draws a card and reads the word. If he reads the word correctly, he places the card, face up, on one of the spaces on the tic-tc-toe game board. If he reads the word incorrectly, he puts the card at the bottom of the word pile. The second player draws a card. If she reads the word correctly, she places it face down on one of the spaces on the tic-tac-toe game board. (Instead of using x's and o's, as in the traditional tic-tac-toe game, the students distinguish their own spaces by placing the cards either face up or face down.) Play continues until one student has placed three word cards in a row vertically, horizontally, or diagonally (to win the game), or until all of the spaces on the board are filled (in which case the game is a draw.)

Variation

Tic-tac-toe can be played with sound cards instead of word cards. Students select a sound card, say the corresponding sound, and place the card on the tic-tac-toe board. They continue as with word cards.

ATTENDANCE LIST

Phonetic Spelling of Name	Segmented Sounds in Name
1.	
2.	
3.	
4.	
5.	
6.	
7.	
8.	
9.	
10.	
11.	
12.	
13.	
14.	
15.	

For Activity 1.1

16. _____   _____

17. _____   _____

18. _____   _____

19. _____   _____

20. _____   _____

21. _____   _____

22. _____   _____

23. _____   _____

24. _____   _____

25. _____   _____

26. _____   _____

27. _____   _____

28. _____   _____

29. _____   _____

30. _____   _____

(page 2 of Attendance List)

LISTS OF CAT...

FAMILY MEMBERS

mother
father
sister
brother
grandma
grandpa
aunt
uncle
cousin

COLORS

red
green
orange
blue
black
white
pink
brown
yellow
purple

I Can...

play the fist game.
sort objects into
       Sounds
· play the fist geme
  t try to write words
· pick words from pile
      and read them

BODY PARTS

leg
arm
ear
eye
mouth
knee
elbow
lips
head
toes

CLOTHIN...

shirt
hat
pants
skirt
dress
scarf
sweater
jeans
belt
mitts

① read + write Room.

② Handwriting
   Computer
③ Raz-kids.
   Starfall.com

plate
bowl

FEELINGS

happy
sad
glad
mad
silly
funny
tired
thirsty
upset

For Activities 1.2 and 1.3

DIRECTIONS

up
down
under
over
beside
above
north
south
west
east

FRUITS AND
VEGETABLES

apple
orange
peach
pear
plum
grapefruit
peas
corn
lettuce
beans

ANIMALS

dog
cat
mouse
cow
horse
pig
sheep
lamb
hen
chick

NUMBERS

one
two
three
four
five
six
seven
eight
nine
ten

WEATHER WORDS

sunny
windy
rainy
clear
cold
hot
warm
cool
snowy
icy

COMMUNITY
HELPERS

teacher
nurse
doctor
baker
butcher
pilot

(page 2 of Lists of Categorized Words)

FIRST/LAST SOUNDS LISTS

WORDS THAT BEGIN WITH THE SAME SOUND

ball	can	dog	fin	girl	hen
bat	keep	door	fur	green	hay
bed	corn	dive	fox	gray	hello
big	cage	date	fine	go	hot
box	camp	dug	fill	gum	hill
bill	cone	damp	fun	give	heart
jug	lip	me	no	pig	run
jar	lime	milk	nap	pet	rat
joke	lamb	move	never	pour	rest
jolt	love	map	nose	pat	ripple
jam	like	mask	nibble	pin	rope
jelly	lost	make	name	pole	rule
sand	take	vote	wind	yo-yo	zebra
soup	teeth	vine	web	yellow	zoo
sun	two	vase	water	yacht	zinc
stamp	ten	violet	window	yawn	zero
spill	test	very	when	yes	zucchini
store	time	vest	why	yolk	zone

WORDS THAT END WITH THE SAME SOUND

web	lick	sad	if	leg	bell
bob	lock	lid	off	pig	hole
robe	sick	and	tough	rag	sell
rub	pack	find	rough	dog	goal
tub	pick	old	cuff	rug	tell
tab	luck	mud	calf	fog	file
rim	can	zip	kiss	cat	love
sum	pen	rope	pass	night	five
numb	pin	pipe	fuss	hat	have
lamb	pine	dip	hiss	bought	hive
hem	main	cape	toss	rat	dove
them	down	hope	mess	bit	gave

ROUND-ROBIN RHYMING LISTS

at	in	it	an	sack	sad
sat	bin	bit	fan	pack	had
cat	fin	fit	man	lack	glad
mat	pin	mit	pan	rack	mad
hat	tin	pit	tan	back	fad
rat	win	sit	ran	tack	bad

am	pig	cape	love	fin
lamb	dig	grape	glove	bin
ham	big	nape	dove	pin
Sam	fig	drape	above	tin
gram	rig	crêpe		

For Activity 1.7

SOUND CARDS FOR THE SIMPLE SOUNDS

SOUND GROUP A

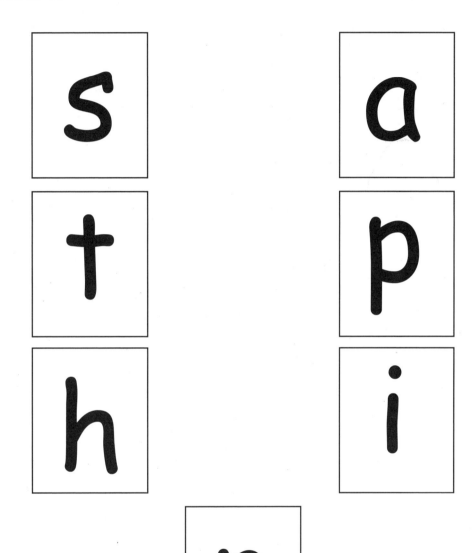

SOUND CARDS FOR THE SIMPLE SOUNDS

SOUND GROUP B

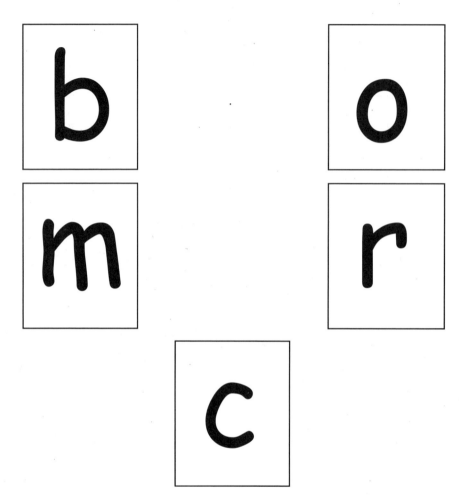

For Activities 2.1 and 2.2, and Lessons 1.2, 1.3, and 1.4

SOUND CARDS FOR THE SIMPLE SOUNDS

SOUND GROUP C

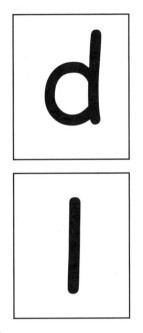

For Activities 2.1 and 2.2, and Lessons 1.2, 1.3, and 1.4

SOUND CARDS FOR THE SIMPLE SOUNDS

SOUND GROUP D

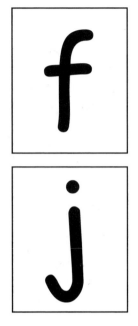

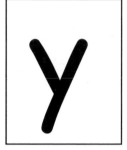

For Activities 2.1 and 2.2, and Lessons 1.2, 1.3, and 1.4

SOUND CARDS FOR THE SIMPLE SOUNDS

SOUND GROUP E

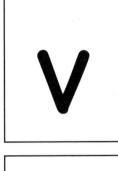

THE SHORT VOWELS

a   e

i   o

u

THE SHORT VOWELS

a   e

i   o

u

For Activity 2.3

REPRODUCIBLE BLANK SOUND CARDS

For Activities 2.2 and 2.4

WORD CARDS FOR THE SIMPLE SOUNDS

SOUND GROUP A

at	an
sat	sap
sip	pat
pit	pin

For Activities 2.5 and 2.6, and Lessons 1.2, 1.4, 1.5, and 1.6

WORD CARDS FOR THE SIMPLE SOUNDS

SOUND GROUP A

tap	tan
tip	tin
hat	hit
hip	nip

WORD CARDS FOR THE SIMPLE SOUNDS

SOUND GROUP A

nap	past
hint	snap
snip	spit
spin	tint

For Activities 2.5 and 2.6, and Lessons 1.2, 1.4, 1.5, and 1.6

WORD CARDS FOR THE SIMPLE SOUNDS

SOUND GROUP B

on	rot
cab	map
ran	man
bit	mob

WORD CARDS FOR THE SIMPLE SOUNDS

SOUND GROUP B

bib	Bob
mop	hot
Ron	rob
pot	cot

For Activities 2.5 and 2.6, and Lessons 1.2, 1.4, 1.5, and 1.6

WORD CARDS FOR THE SIMPLE SOUNDS

SOUND GROUP B

hop	rip
rat	spot
ramp	cram
crib	brat

For Activities 2.5 and 2.6, and Lessons 1.2, 1.4, 1.5, and 1.6

WORD CARDS FOR THE SIMPLE SOUNDS

SOUND GROUP B

scrap	stop
cramp	stomp
stamp	camp
crab	trap

For Activities 2.5 and 2.6, and Lessons 1.2, 1.4, 1.5, and 1.6

WORD CARDS FOR THE SIMPLE SOUNDS

SOUND GROUP C

get	red
sad	hid
lid	got
big	bad

WORD CARDS FOR THE SIMPLE SOUNDS

SOUND GROUP C

log	leg
dip	let
dog	bed
lot	grip

For Activities 2.5 and 2.6, and Lessons 1.2, 1.4, 1.5, and 1.6

WORD CARDS FOR THE SIMPLE SOUNDS

SOUND GROUP C

brag	slob
grim	plop
glad	help
slap	stem

For Activities 2.5 and 2.6, and Lessons 1.2, 1.4, 1.5, and 1.6

WORD CARDS FOR THE SIMPLE SOUNDS

SOUND GROUP C

sled	slip
grasp	strap
brand	print
grab	grin

For Activities 2.5 and 2.6, and Lessons 1.2, 1.4, 1.5, and 1.6

WORD CARDS FOR THE SIMPLE SOUNDS

SOUND GROUP D

fun	yet
us	jet
yes	fog
up	fin

WORD CARDS FOR THE SIMPLE SOUNDS

SOUND GROUP D

jug	jog
run	jab
fit	ram
flag	flip

For Activities 2.5 and 2.6, and Lessons 1.2, 1.4, 1.5, and 1.6

WORD CARDS FOR THE SIMPLE SOUNDS

SOUND GROUP D

fast	frog
glum	slug
jump	yelp
gulp	drum

WORD CARDS FOR THE SIMPLE SOUNDS

SOUND GROUP D

gum	rut
Gus	just
flat	flint
fact	fund

For Activities 2.5 and 2.6, and Lessons 1.2, 1.4, 1.5, and 1.6

WORD CARDS FOR THE SIMPLE SOUNDS

SOUND GROUP D

film	plug
plum	job
mud	jot
flap	flip

For Activities 2.5 and 2.6, and Lessons 1.2, 1.4, 1.5, and 1.6

WORD CARDS FOR THE SIMPLE SOUNDS

SOUND GROUP E

ax	zip
six	Oz
fax	zig
zag	wet

For Activities 2.5 and 2.6, and Lessons 1.2, 1.4, 1.5, and 1.6

WORD CARDS FOR THE SIMPLE SOUNDS

SOUND GROUP E

wit	vet
van	web
fox	wax
box	yam

WORD CARDS FOR THE SIMPLE SOUNDS

SOUND GROUP E

yak	wig
zap	tax
vest	rest
wind	exit

For Activities 2.5 and 2.6, and Lessons 1.2, 1.4, 1.5, and 1.6

WORD CARDS FOR THE SIMPLE SOUNDS

SOUND GROUP E

west	twig
vent	wept
wisp	welt
went	wilt

TIC-TAC-TOE GAME BOARD

For Activity 2.6

4

Lesson Plans for Small Groups or Individuals

In this chapter, we present a series of easy-to-follow, logically sequenced lesson plans that are designed to teach phonemic awareness, decoding skills, and encoding skills. The chapter is divided into three parts. **Part 1** contains systematic sound-symbol correspondences for the simple sounds: that is, those sounds that are represented by one-to-one mapping patterns (one letter = one sound). Once students have mastered blending, segmenting, decoding, and encoding two- to six-phoneme words containing one-to-one mapping patterns and they are able to differentiate short-vowel sounds, they will be ready to move on to the lessons in part 2.

Part 2 contains an introduction to the consonant digraphs *sh, th, ch,* and *ck*. Here, students will have opportunities to apply their blending and segmenting skills to words containing two-to-one mapping patterns (two letters used to represent one sound).

Part 3 introduces complex-vowel digraphs. Students will learn to recognize *vowel-consonant-e* spelling patterns (for example, *o-consonant-e* spells the sound /oa/) and combinations of letters that represent a single sound (for example, the letters *igh*, which represent the sound /ie/). They will also learn that the same sound can be represented a variety of different ways (for example, the sound /ay/ can be spelled *a-consonant-e, ai,* and *ay*).

This volume is intended to be a guide to linking phonemic awareness to decoding and encoding; however, we do not systematically introduce every possible spelling pattern of every single sound. Through our work with hundreds of students over the past decade and a half, we have determined that such an approach is neither necessary nor desirable. Once students master blending and segmenting and are taught spelling patterns for the various sounds (including consonant and vowel digraphs), they begin to develop a fundamental understanding of how the alphabetic code functions to represent speech sounds. Students learn that flexibility in decoding and encoding is the key to success: if a word does not sound right, they learn

Jason was one of the best segmenters in Heather's kindergarten class. One afternoon during journal-writing time, Jason approached Heather and asked, "Mrs. Kenny, how do you spell the sound /oo/?" Knowing that the spelling of sounds can be word-specific, Heather asked, "What word are you spelling?" "Book," replied Jason. "The sound /oo/ in the word *book* is spelled *oo*," Heather responded. Jason hurried back to his seat and resumed writing, spelling the word *boock*.

Although he had not spelled the word "correctly," Jason demonstrated a sophisticated understanding of encoding. He was astute enough to recognize /oo/ as a sound and ask how to spell that sound. In addition, he demonstrated an understanding of digraphs by recording the letters *oo* without question and using the letters *ck* (a common spelling pattern for /k/ in the final position). Although the rest of the class was not yet ready for this information, Heather took advantage of a "teachable moment" and introduced Jason to the complex spelling pattern of a new sound. Thereafter, his journal entries were peppered with *oo*'s whenever he came across a word containing the sound /oo/.

to try a different phoneme. If a word does not look right, they learn to try a different spelling pattern. As a teacher, you need to take advantage of "teachable moments" to fill in any gaps in your students' knowledge. If, for example, a student were struggling with the word *straight*, you could simply cue him by saying, "The letters *aigh* spell the sound /ay/." (See Lesson 1.7, pages 97 and 98)

The lessons we present here are appropriate for use with both small groups and individuals; thus, they are ideal for use with students who receive special-education or English-language support on a withdrawal basis, as well as for students who receive one-on-one tutoring. The small-group instructional format can also be incorporated into a classroom setting. You can easily divide students into groups of five or six and direct the students to rotate through a series of language-based centers while you remain at one center and guide the students through the lessons. Alternately, you might adapt the lessons for use with an entire class.

You need not complete the lessons daily (but you could if you chose to). They can be highly effective when presented one to three times per week. Base your decision about frequency on the needs of your students and your own planning preferences.

In order to plan for appropriate instruction, it is important that you first assess your students' phonemic awareness and alphabetic coding skills. For students in kindergarten and the beginning of first grade, such an assessment need not take the form of a test. Instead, you as the teacher can carefully observe individual students during whole-group phonemic awareness games and activities (such as those described in chapter 3). However, if you are unfamiliar with the types of activities recommended in this book, it will take time before you become proficient at blending and segmenting confidently. But, once you become comfortable with this approach to teaching reading and spelling, you will quickly pick up on which students are able to blend and segment simple, and even more complex, words. These are the children who are focused and fully engaged during phonemic awareness games. They look directly at you with eager, expectant faces and watch your mouth carefully, often forming the sounds along with you. They extend their fingers as they segment, and they pinch them together as they blend. They are the first to call out answers in strong, clear, confident voices.

Then there are the students who will require extra modeling and support. They are likely the children who prefer to sit at the back of the room or on the fringes of the group. Their expressions may be blank or their brows furrowed in concentration. Their eyes may wander around the classroom or dart from you to their peers. They may watch their classmates carefully, to see how they are responding, then mimic the other children's behaviors.

These are the students who typically call out the answers half a beat behind the others, or not at all. They are the children who must rely on the rest of the group to shout out their names during daily attendance activities before they feel confident raising their own hands. You can make these observations discreetly during the course of the activities and note them quietly.

If you feel that a more formal assessment is in order, consider using the Phonemic Awareness Assessment provided on pages 107 to 110. Although this assessment may be used selectively as a pretest with students as young as six, we feel that it is generally more appropriately administered after students have had some phonemic awareness instruction. Remember that many children in the early primary grades may have had little or no experience blending and segmenting. And some of these younger students may be unfamiliar with concepts such as *sound, word,* and *nonsense word.*

For students in first grade and for struggling decoders in second grade and beyond, it is crucial that teachers assess both the phonemic awareness and the alphabetic coding skills of the students before starting instruction. Teachers need a thorough understanding of what these students know (or do not know) and can do (or cannot do). The Phonemic Awareness Assessment and the Alphabetic Coding Assessment (see pages 111 to 115) are both quick and easy to administer, and they provide valuable information that can help you plan appropriate interventions. Heather administered these assessments to Carolyn, a student with whom she worked privately.

Carolyn was a soft-spoken, yet articulate, student who began working with Heather at the beginning of her eighth-grade year. Though she was obviously intelligent, Carolyn had been diagnosed with a learning disability and was reading several grade levels below eighth grade. At their first meeting, Heather administered three assessments. First, Heather asked Carolyn to read several paragraphs of an appropriate text. When it became evident that Carolyn struggled to identify words correctly, Heather administered two more assessments—versions of the Phonemic Awareness Assessment and the Alphabetic Coding Assessment. (See figures 4.1 and 4.2 for Carolyn's responses to the two tests. Note that the student responses indicated in these figures are based on a composite profile of a student. Although the responses do not show actual student work, they reflect the abilities of actual eight-grade students.)

Note that Carolyn's responses in part 1 (Blending) of the Phonemic Awareness Assessment indicate that, while she was able to blend and segment simple vowel-consonant (VC) and consonant-vowel-consonant (CVC) words, she had difficulty with words that contained adjacent consonants in the final position, or in the initial and final positions. Carolyn's inability to blend and segment sounds hindered her ability to decode and encode, making it

PHONEMIC AWARENESS ASSESSMENT

PART 1: BLENDING

Test Items	Student Response	Correct Response
1. /r/-/ee/	✓	ree
2. /e/-/k/	✓	eck
3. /l/-/i/-/g/	✓	lig
4. /p/-/a/-/b/	✓	pab
5. /s/-/m/-/ie/	✓	smy
6. /g/-/l/-/o/-/g/	✓	glog
7. /t/-/u/-/s/-/p/	*tups*	tusp
8. /d/-/a/-/c/-/t/	*dack*	dact
9. /c/-/l/-/or/-/s/	✓	clors
10. /f/-/r/-/i/-/m/-/p/	*frip*	frimp
11. /b/-/l/-/ee/-/n/-/d/	*bleed*	bleend
12. /s/-/t/-/r/-/oo/-/ck/	*strook*	strook

Student's score ___7___ divided by 12 = .58 x 100 = 58 %

Figure 4.1: Carolyn's responses to the Phonemic Awareness Assessment

difficult for her to identify unknown words when reading or to recall correct letter sequences when spelling.

The results of Carolyn's Alphabetic Coding Assessment were also a cause for concern. While she breezed through part 1 (Consonants), Carolyn experienced difficulty discriminating between the short vowel sounds /e/ and /i/, not surprising, since they are the most difficult sounds in the English language to distinguish between. Struggling readers frequently have difficulty distinguishing between /e/ and /i/ or between /o/ and /u/.

As well, when Carolyn responded to items such as those in parts 3 (Consonant Diagraphs), and 4 (Vowel Diagraphs), she was unable to correctly identify the sounds that were represented by graphemes such as *wr* and *eigh*. Instead, she provided words that contained the corresponding spelling patterns (*write* and *eight* respectively). Obviously, Carolyn recognized the letter combinations from words in her sight-word vocabulary. What she did not recognize was why those letter combinations were present in those

PHONEMIC AWARENESS ASSESSMENT

PART 2: SEGMENTING

Test Items	Student Response	Correct Response
1. ep	✓ - ✓	/e/ - /p/
2. tay	✓ - ✓	/t/ - /ay/
3. lat	✓ - ✓ - ✓	/l/ - /a/ - /t/
4. jick	✓ - ✓ - ✓	/j/ - /i/ - /k/
5. spim	✓ - ✓ - ✓ - ✓	/s/ - /p/ - /i/ - /m/
6. drot	✗ - ✗ - ✓ - ✓	/d/ - /r/ - /o/ - /t/
7. bisp	✓ - ✓ - ✗ - ✗	/b/ - /i/ - /s/ - /p/
8. hant	✓ - ✗ - ✗ - ✗	/h/ - /a/ - /n/ - /t/
9. ployd	✓ - ✓ - ✗ - ✗	/p/ - /l/ - /oy/ - /d/
10. grost	✓ - ✓ - ✗ - ✗ - ✗	/g/ - /r/ - /o/ - /s/ - /t/
11. clind	✗ - ✗ - ✓ - ✗ - ✗	/c/ - /l/ - /i/ - /n/ - /d/
12. strump	✗ - ✗ - ✗ - ✗ - ✓ - ✓	/s/ - /t/ - /r/ - /u/ - /m/ - /p/

Student's score _26_ divided by 46 = _.565_ x 100 = _56.5_ %

(Figure 4.1 continued)

words. She did not know (and had never been taught) that *wr* is an acceptable spelling pattern for the sound /r/ or that *eigh* represents the sound /ay/. To Carolyn, these spelling patterns were not patterns at all; they were arbitrary sequences of letters that had to be memorized in the correct order.

The information that these last two assessments provided enabled Heather to build an effective program for Carolyn. For 30 minutes, once a week, Heather focused on developing Carolyn's phonemic awareness skills and teaching Carolyn to discriminate between /i/ and /e/. She also taught her how to blend and segment words containing adjacent consonants. As well, Heather systematically introduced Carolyn to complex spelling patterns (such as those in part 3 of this chapter), and she helped Carolyn practice decoding and encoding words containing all of these patterns. By the end of the academic year, Carolyn could quickly and accurately decode almost any word that she encountered, and she was able to read and comprehend grade-level text. Her spelling skills, while not perfect, had also dramatically improved.

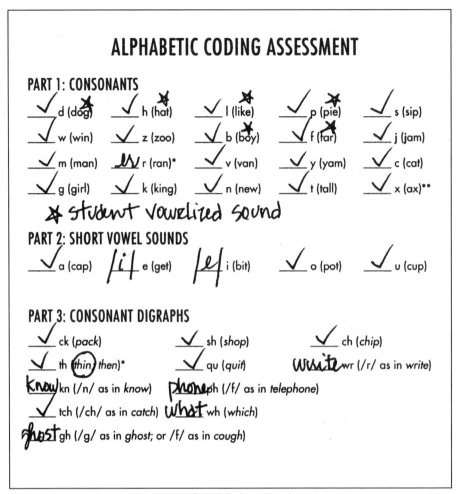

Figure 4.2: Carolyn's responses to the Alphabetic Coding Assessment.

PART 1: SEVEN LESSONS FOR TEACHING THE SIMPLE SOUNDS

The seven lessons provided in this section are fun and easy to implement. Follow them sequentially and you will systematically teach your students how to decode (read) and to encode (spell) words containing simple sounds (one-to-one mapping patterns). We introduce the simple sounds in a series of five sound groups. You will find these sound groups, the word lists for each lesson, and the order in which they are to be taught in the reproducible master entitled Order for Teaching the Simple Sounds, which is found on pages 116 and 117. The lessons in this section are equally effective with beginning readers and struggling readers—those who have not developed strong decoding and encoding skills.

Start with lesson 1.1 to teach the first sound and repeat it for each of the remaining sounds in the sound group (A). Once you have introduced all of the sounds in the sound group, have the students engage in the remaining six lessons. Repeat this procedure for the remaining sounds in the sound group.

PART 4: VOWEL DIGRAPHS

✓ ___ or (/or/ as in "fork"; /er/ as in "work")

✓ ___ er (/er/ as in "verb")

✓ ___ ea (/ee/ as in "meat"; /e/ as in "bread"; /ay/ as in "great")

✓ ___ ir (/er/ as in "fir")

✓ ___ oa (/oa/ as in "coat")

hurt ___ ur (/er/ as in "fur")

✓ ___ ee (/ee/ as in "meet")

✓ ___ ie (/ie/ as in "pie"; /ee/ as in "thief")

✓ ___ ay (/ay/ as in "day")

✓ ___ ey (/ee/ as in "monkey"; /ay/ as in "they")

P ___ ou (/ow/ as in "couch"; /u/ as in "touch"; /oo/ as in "troupe")

✓ ___ ai (/ay/ as in "paid"; /e/ as in "said")

P ___ oi (/oy/ as in "oil")

cow ___ ow (/ow/ as in "cow"; /oa/ as in "snow")

boy ___ oy (/oy/ as in "toy")

P ___ oo (/oo/ as in "soon"; /oo/ as in "look')

P ___ oe (/oa/ as in "doe"; /oo/ as in "shoe")

autumn ___ au (/o/ as in "August")

P ___ ew (/oo/ as in "crew"; /ue/ as in "cue")

P ___ aw (/o/ as in "paw")

P ___ ui (/oo/ as in "ruin")

light ___ igh (/ie/ as in "sigh")

P ___ ough (/o/ as in "thought"; /oo/ as in "through"; /oa/ as in "thorough")

P ___ augh (/o/ as in "taught")

light ___ eigh (/ay/ as in "eight")

(Figure 4.2 continued)

We recommend that you follow the order presented in Order for Teaching the Simple Sounds, pages 116 and 117.

Do not rush through the lessons. Rather, provide ample time for your students to learn, practice, and master the skills. Repeat the lessons as needed. Pay particular attention to your students' abilities to discriminate among the short-vowel sounds, and make sure that they have mastered the ability to blend and segment words with adjacent consonants in both the initial and final positions. Once your students have mastered simple one-to-one mapping patterns and they can quickly and accurately blend, segment, decode, and encode single-syllable words with up to six phonemes, they will be ready to tackle the more complex elements of the alphabetic code found in parts 2 and 3.

For kindergarten and early first-grade students, most of whom have not yet learned all the sound-symbol correspondences, we recommend that you follow the lessons sequentially, as presented here, starting with lesson 1.1. Many older readers and spellers, and even some who are struggling, may already have mastered the sound-symbol correspondences for the simple sounds. In such cases, it would be appropriate to merely undertake a quick review of the sounds (to ensure that students are pronouncing them correctly), then skip to lesson 1.2. In all cases, however, we strongly recommend that you introduce the kinesthetic cues (see the action pages provided in the appendix, pages 203 to 228) for any sound-symbol correspondences that students have not yet mastered, particularly the short-vowel sounds.

Once you have completed all seven lessons for a sound group, you may wish to assess your students' mastery of the skills they have been practising. Use the reproducible masters entitled Phonemic Awareness and the Alphabetic Coding assessments found on pages 107 to 115.

Lesson 1.1: Phonemic Awareness Training

Complete lesson 1.1 for each sound in sound group *A* (*s, a, t, p, h, i, n*) before continuing with the rest of the lessons.

Materials

- one action page (placed in a highly visible spot in the classroom) for the sound being taught and all previously introduced sounds

- a pictures page for the sound being taught (one copy per student)

- a words-and-pictures page for the sound being taught (one copy per student)

- story starters for the sound being taught (for the teacher)

- riddles for the sound being taught (for the teacher)

Find reproducible masters for action pages, pictures pages, and words-and-pictures pages in the appendix at the end of this book. Find story starters and riddles in the appendix, pages 190 to 202.

Instructions

Step 1: Review each sound/symbol taught to date. For example, show the symbol *s* on the action page:

Teacher (The teacher points to the letter *s*.) Which sound does the letter *s* spell?

Students /s/

Continue with all other sounds-symbols taught to date.

Step 2: Introduce the new sound-symbol. Show students the action page for the new sound. Demonstrate the sound-action combination. You may choose to have very young students dramatize a story associated with the sound. For example:

Teacher Imagine that you have a pet snake named Sammy. You go up to your room and notice that the snake is missing. You look under the chair. No Sammy. You look in the closet. No Sammy. Then you hear "ssss." (The teacher waves her arms in the air like a snake as she says the sound.) You look under your bed, and there is /s/, /s/, Sammy.

Repeat the sound-action combination several times with students.

Step 3: Play a riddle game for the sound being taught. Distribute one pictures page per student. Introduce the vocabulary on the page by asking riddles. For example:

Teacher I'm thinking of a word that begins with the sound /s/. I am a ball of fire and gas. I shine brightly in the sky. Plants and animals need me to grow. What am I?

Students sun (The students point to the sun.)

Repeat with other riddles for the remaining words.

Step 4: Play a rhyming game. Still referring to the pictures pages, make up words or non-words that rhyme with the words on the page. For example:

Teacher I'm thinking of a word that rhymes with *car*.

Students star (The students point to a picture of a star.)

Teacher I'm thinking of a word that rhymes with *fider*.

Students spider

Repeat with remaining words on the pictures pages.

Step 5: Have students blend the sounds in words. Still referring to the pictures page, segment the sounds in two-to-four-phoneme words and ask students to blend them. For example:

RESEARCH TO PRACTICE

While teaching kindergarten and first grade, Laura noticed that her students loved riddles. She allowed her students to make up their own riddles and present them to their classmates. It was fun, highly motivating, and an effective way to promote both oral language and higher-level thinking skills.

blend

segment

Teacher	I am going to say each sound in a word. I want you to say the word and touch the picture: /s/ /u/ /n/. (The teacher allows a one-second interval between sounds.)
Students	sun (The students touch a picture of the sun.)

Repeat using other pictures on the page that contain two to four sounds. For a challenge, invite students to blend words containing more than four phonemes.

Step 6: Have students segment the sounds in words. Still referring to the pictures page, say a two-to- four-phoneme word and instruct them to segment each sound in that word. Provide modeling and assistance as needed. For example:

Teacher	I am going to say each sound in the word *sun*. I want you to hold up one finger for each sound: /s/ /u/ /n/. (The students each extend one finger for each sound.) How many sounds are in the word *sun*?
Students	three
Teacher	Now, say each sound in the word *sun*.
Students	/s/ /u/ /n/ (The students each extend one finger for each sound.) sun (pinching fingers together)

Repeat using other pictures on the page that contain two to four sounds.

Step 7: Have students record the letter that spells the sound on the pictures page. For example, invite them to print the letter symbol *s* three times on the line beside each picture, saying /s/ aloud as they print the letter.

Distribute the words and pictures pages and invite students to circle the letter that spells the target sound in the words. For example:

Teacher	Circle the letter that spells the sound /s/ in *spider*. (The teacher says the sound but not the letter name.)
Students	/s/ (The students circle the letter *s*.)

Repeat with other words on the page.

Extensions

Extension 1: As students learn more sound-symbol combinations, you may choose to have them identify other, previously taught, sounds. Have them circle the medial and/or final sounds on the words-and-pictures page. For example:

Teacher	What is the second sound in the word *star*: /s/…?

What sound does this letter spell

Students	/t/
Teacher	Circle the letter that spells the sound /t/ in the word *star*.

Extension 2: Introduce complex spellings of sounds. For example:

Teacher	What is the last sound in the word *star*: /s/-/t/…?
Students	/ar/
Teacher	There are two letters that spell the sound /ar/ in the word *star*. Which two letters spell the sound /ar/?
Students	ar
Teacher	Circle the letters *ar* in the word *star*.

Repeat lesson 1.1 for each sound in the sound group before moving on to the remaining six lessons.

Lesson 1.2: Word Building

Materials

- a plastic zip-lock bag containing sound cards for each of the sounds in the sound group being taught and sound cards for those previously taught (one per student)

- word cards for the sound group being taught

- chalk and chalkboard

- a pencil and some paper for each student

Find sound cards for the simple sounds and word cards for the simple sounds as reproducible masters at the end of chapter 3, pages 55 to 81. Find the word list for lesson 1.2 on pages 116 and 117.

Instructions

Step 1: Review each sound-symbol taught to date. Model the spellings of words. For example:

Teacher	Let's count the sounds in the word *at*: /a/-/t/, at. (The teacher extends one finger for each sound.) What is the first sound you hear in the word *at*?
Students	/t/ (The teacher records the letter *t* on the chalkboard while saying the sound /t/.) (The teacher pinches her fingers to indicate to the students that they should blend the word.) at
Teacher	What is the next sound you hear in the word *at*? /a/…?

| Students | /t/ (The teacher records the letter *t* on the chalkboard while saying the sound /t/.) |

Repeat using other words from the word list.

Step 2: Have students build words with sound cards. For example:

| Teacher | Using your sound cards, build the word *at*. Say each sound out loud as you build the word. |
| Students | /a/-/t/ (The students place the appropriate card on the table as they say each sound.) at |

Repeat using other words from the word list.

Step 3: Have students record words. Provide each student with a pencil and some paper and instruct them to print out each sound in the words that they hear. For example:

Teacher	Tell me each sound you hear in the word *at*.
Students	/a/-/t/, at
Teacher	Spell the word *at*. Say each sound out loud as you read it. (The students record the word, saying each sound aloud as it is recorded.)

Repeat using other words from the word list.

Lesson 1.3: Manipulating Sounds

Materials

- a plastic zip-lock bag containing sound cards for the simple sounds for each of the sounds taught to date (one per student)

- the word list for lesson 1.3

- chalk and chalkboard

- a pencil and some paper for each student

Find sound cards for the simple sounds and word cards for the simple sounds as reproducible masters at the end of chapter 3, pages 55 to 81. Find the word list for lesson 1.3 on pages 116 and 117.

Instructions

Step 1: Review each sound-symbol taught to date. Spell the sounds in the first word on the list. For example:

Lesson 1.6: Spelling Practice for the Simple Sounds

Materials

- word list for the sound group being taught (select words from the appropriate lists on pages 116 and 117)

- a pencil and a piece of paper for each student

Instructions

Give your students a spelling "test." (This activity could be an actual test, intended to assess students' mastery of the new sound, or it could be an opportunity to provide students with extra practice. In the latter case, you might wish to have the entire group segment the words aloud before the students record them.) Call out one word at a time, encouraging the students to segment it out loud and then record the sounds, saying each sound aloud as they record it. For example:

Teacher	Tell me the sounds in the word *in.*
Students	/i/-/n/, in
Teacher	Spell each sound in the word *in.* Say each sound out loud, then record the letters, saying each sound aloud as they record the corresponding letter.

Continue with eight to 10 other words on the word list. As your students' proficiency increases, you may choose to increase the number of words.

Lesson 1.7: Building Fluency for the Simple Sounds

Materials

- a variety of reading materials, including fiction, nonfiction, poems, songs, readers' theater scripts, graphic novels

- bins for organizing and storing texts

Instructions

Have students practice reading texts at their independent levels. Encourage them to select texts based on their individual interests and independent reading levels. Provide them with 15 to 20 minutes of uninterrupted time to read independently. If a student finishes one text within the time period, invite him or her to reread the same text or select another. (For additional activities designed to promote reading fluency, see Rasinski.)

It is important to encourage students to use their decoding skills in the classroom context when they are reading actual books or stories, not just contrived texts. When they encounter unfamiliar words or sounds, encourage them to make a phonetic approximation and then attempt to self-correct, based on context cues. (For a discussion of phonetic approximations, see pages 26, 30, and 31.) By attending to the meaning of words, your students will improve their self-monitoring skills, which can ultimately improve their reading comprehension.

If, however, a student still struggles with a word, provide the sound unit with which he or she is struggling. For example, if a student comes across the word *right* but has not been taught that the letters *igh* represent the sound /ie/ as in *pie*, simply tell him or her the sound:

Teacher	Say the sounds in that word out loud.
Student	/r/
Teacher	The letters *igh* spell the sound /ie/.
Student	/r/ - /ie/ - /t/. Right.

Once students have completed lessons 1.1 to 1.7 for the sound group, you might wish to assess you students' mastery of the concepts by administering the Phonemic Awareness Assessment and the Alphabetic Coding Assessment for the appropriate sound group (find these as reproducible masters on pages 107 to 115). If the students are ready, move on to the next sound group, or, if your students have completed the lessons for all the sound groups, move on to the lessons in part 2.

PART 2: FOUR LESSONS FOR TEACHING CONSONANT DIGRAPHS

In part 1, we provided lesson plans that teach students simple elements of the alphabetic code: one-to-one mapping patterns. Students learned that an individual phoneme can be represented by a single letter, and they learn to blend, segment, decode, and encode words that employ one-to-one mapping patterns. In part 2, we provide lesson plans that introduce two-to-one mapping patterns (two letters = one sound): consonant digraphs. Students learn that a single sound can be represented by more than one letter (for example, the letters *sh* are used to spell the sound /sh/), and they practice decoding and encoding words containing those digraphs. Since these spelling patterns (sh, ch, th, and ck) are rarely problematic for students, we have devoted only four lessons to teaching each of the consonant digraphs. Let your students guide you. If they appear to need additional practice, repeat the lessons as needed. Complete the four lessons for the sound /sh/, then repeat them, in order, for the digraphs /ch/, /th/, and /ck/.

Once you have completed the lessons for all four consonant digraphs, you might wish to assess your students' mastery of the skills they have been practicing. Use the reproducible master entitled Assessment for Consonant Digraphs found on pages 133 and 134.

Lesson 2.1: Spelling the Consonant Digraph

Materials

- a spelling-the-sound sheet for the consonant digraph being taught (one copy per student)
- a copy of the spelling-the-sound sheet for the sound being taught reprinted on chart paper or on an overhead transparency
- chart paper or overhead transparency

Find reproducible masters for spelling-the-sound sheets for the consonant diagraphs between pages 135 and 146.

Instructions

Step 1: Introduce the new sound. For example:

Teacher	We are going to learn to read and spell words that contain the sound /sh/. Let's practice saying the sound /sh/.
Students	/sh/
Teacher	(The teacher refers to the chart paper or overhead.) The first word on our list is *ship*. Listen to the sounds in the word *ship*: /sh/ /i/ /p/. Now, say the word *ship*.
Students	ship
Teacher	Let's say the sounds in the word *ship*.
Students and Teacher	/sh/ /i/ /p/, ship

Continue with remaining words on the word list.

Step 2: Have students segment each word and record each sound in the word on the blank lines found beside each word on the spelling-the-sounds sheet. You may wish to have students circle or underline the spelling of the new sound in each word.

Lesson 2.2: Reinforcement Games for Consonant Digraphs

Materials

- multiple sets of word cards for the consonant digraph being taught; find reproducible masters for these between pages 135 and 146

- additional materials, as described in chapter 3, related to the games listed in this lesson

Instructions

Prepare playing cards by cutting out the individual word cards and laminating them. Provide students with an opportunity to develop and consolidate their skills by giving them the word cards for the new sound and having them play one of the following games. Students may play the games in pairs or in small groups.

- go fishing for sounds (see page 44)

- sound concentration (see page 44)

- beat the clock (see page 47)

- tic-tac-toe (see page 47)

- what's in the middle? (see page 45)

Extension

Place these games at a literacy center for student use during free-choice-activity time.

Lesson 2.3: Spelling Practice for Consonant Digraphs

Materials

- a word list for the consonant digraph being taught (compile the word list from words on the word cards for the consonant digraph being taught) (for teacher reference only); find reproducible masters for these between pages 136 and 146

- a pencil and some paper for each student

Instructions

Give your students a spelling "test." (This activity could be an actual test, intended to assess students' mastery of the new sound, or it could be an opportunity to provide students with extra practice. In the latter case, you might wish to have the entire group segment the words aloud before they record them.) Call out one word at a time, encouraging students to segment the word as they record the sounds saying each sound aloud as they record it. For example:

Teacher   Spell each sound in the word *ship*.

Students   /sh/-/i/ /p/ (the students record the word *ship*), ship

Continue with the remaining words on the spelling-the-sound sheet.

Lesson 2.4: Building Fluency for the Consonant Digraphs

Materials

- a variety of reading materials, including fiction, nonfiction, poems, songs, readers' theater scripts, graphic novels

- bins for organizing and storing texts

Instructions

Have students practice reading and rereading texts at their independent levels. (For additional activities designed to promote reading fluency, see Rasinski.)

Once students have completed lessons 2.1 to 2.4 for each of the consonant digraphs, you might wish to assess your students' mastery of the concepts by administering the Assessment for Consonant Digraphs (pages 133 and 134). If the students are ready, move on the the lessons in part 3.

PART 3: SIX LESSONS FOR TEACHING VOWEL DIGRAPHS

In part 2, we introduced the concept that a single sound could be represented by more than one letter (a digraph). In part 3, we show that a single sound can be represented in a variety of different ways, and we introduce common spelling patterns for each vowel sound or sound unit. For example, the sound /ay/ can be spelled with the letters *ai* (as in the word *wait*), the letters *ay* (as in the word *day*), and the letters *a–consonant–e* (as in the word *cake*). The lessons in this section build upon the blending and segmenting skills that students have already mastered, and they directly teach students how to apply their knowledge of decoding and encoding to words that contain complex sounds and spelling patterns. We recommend that you present lessons 3.1 to 3.6 for each sound and introduce the sounds in the following order: /er/, /or/, /ar/, /ay/, /ee/, /ie/, /oa/, /ue/, /oo/ (as in *book*), /ow/ (as in *cow*), /oi/, /oo/ (as in *soon*), and the sound units *air* and *ear*. (While we recognize that *air* and *ear* are not individual phonemes, students—and teachers—can experience difficulty segmenting them. We have therefore included these sound units in the lessons.)

Lesson 3.1: Spelling the Vowel Digraph

Materials

- word cards for vowel digraph being taught (one set per group); find reproducible masters for these between pages 148 and 187

```
Name  Lauren T.                    Date  Oct. 30th

SPELLING-SOUNDS SORTING MAT FOR THE SOUND  /ai/

| a – e | ai | ay |
|-------|-----|-----|
| cape  | rain | pay |
| made  | sail | play |
| late  | snail | may |
| name  | wait | say |
```

Figure 4.3: Sample showing how students record words on a spelling-sounds sorting mat

At the end of Laura's very first phonemically driven spelling lesson in a first-grade classroom, a parent volunteer approached Laura with a strong concern about the spelling program. Since the phonemically driven approach was so different from the traditional "rote" method of teaching spelling that she knew, the parent wondered what Laura was doing. Laura quickly explained her rationale and invited the parent to observe the lessons. By the end of the first week, the parent was a convert, declaring that the approach made perfect sense.

- a spelling-the-sound sheet for the vowel digraph being taught, reprinted on chart paper or an overhead transparency; find these as reproducible masters between pages 147 and 185

- chart paper or overhead transparency

Instructions

Step 1: Introduce the new sound. For example:

Teacher	(The teacher refers to the spelling-the-sound sheet on chart paper or overhead transparency.) This week, our spelling words all contain the sound /er/. Let's practice saying the sound /er/.
Students	/er/
Teacher	I am going to count the sounds in the word *her*. Listen: /h/ /er/. Now, say the word *her*. Let's say the sounds together: /h/ /er/, her.

Continue with the remaining words on the chart.

Step 2: Introduce multiple spelling patterns. For example:

Teacher   The sound /er/ can be spelled with the letters, *er, ur,* and *ir.* Let's look at our spelling list (refer to chart paper or overhead). The sounds in the word *her* are /h/-/er/.

Step 3: Record the sounds in the word *her* beside the word on the chart paper or overhead transparency (see sample, figure 4.3).

Teacher   In the word *her,* the sound /er /is spelled with the letters *e* and *r.* Now let's listen to the sounds in the word *sir:* /s/ /ir/. (The teacher segments and records *sir* beside the word *sir* on the chart paper.) Now, say the word *sir.*

Students   sir

Teacher   Let's count the sounds together. (The teacher extends one finger for each sound as she counts.)

Students   /s/ /ir/, sir

Arrange students in small groups and provide each group with a set of word cards for the vowel digraph being taught. Instruct the students to take turns drawing a card, reading the word, and leading the group in segmenting each sound in the word.

Lesson 3.2: Sorting by Spelling Patterns

Materials

- word cards for the vowel digraph being taught (one set per group); find reproducible masters for these between pages 148 and 187

- spelling-sounds sorting mat (one per group); find this as a reproducible master on page 188 (if you wish, use a photocopier to enlarge it to 11" x 14")

- a copy of the spelling-the-sound sheet for the vowel digraph being taught, reprinted on chart paper or overhead transparency

Instructions

Have students sort cards according to the spelling of the sounds. Prepare playing cards by cutting out the individual word cards and laminating them. Make a pile. Pass out a spelling-sounds sorting mat to each student and instruct them as follows:

Teacher   Today we're going to sort words according to the spelling of our new sound. Which new sound did we learn?

Student   /er/

Teacher	Right! Let's write that sound at the top of the page. (The teacher writes /er/ in the appropriate place on his or her sorting mat, and one student in each group does the same on their copy.) The sound /er/ can be spelled with *er, ir,* or *ur.* Let's write in those spellings. (The teacher writes each of the spelling patterns at the top of his or her column, and one student in each group does the same on their copy.)

Draw the top card from the pile of word cards and hold it up so that the students can see it. For example:

Teacher	The first word is *her.* The sounds in the word her are /h/ /er/. How is the sound /er/ in the word *her* spelled?
Student	e…r
Teacher	I'm going to put the word *her* under the heading er on my sorting mat. (The teacher writes *her* in the appropriate column.) Now I want you to use your word cards to sort each word according to the way the sound /er/ is spelled.

Have your students work in pairs or small groups to sort the word cards according to the spelling of the selected sound and place the words in the appropriate column on their sorting mats. For additional practice, encourage students to orally segment and read each word aloud before sorting.

Lesson 3.3: Segmenting and Recording Words

Materials

- a spelling-the-sounds sheet for the vowel digraph being taught (one copy per student); find reproducible masters for these between pages 147 and 184

- spelling-sounds sorting mat (one copy per student); find a reproducible master for this on page 188

Instructions

RESEARCH TO PRACTICE

Students particularly enjoy playing the sound-sorting game. This "hands-on" activity is appealing and equally beneficial to visual, auditory, and kinesthetic learners.

Have students record words according to the spellings of the sounds. Provide each student with a spelling-the-sound sheet for the appropriate sound and a spelling-sounds sorting mat. Instruct students to (1) read the list of words; (2) segment each word into individual sounds; (3) spell the sounds on the lines beside each word; (4) circle the letters that spell the new sound in each word; (5) write each word in the appropriate column on the sorting mat.

Note that the sounds /ay/, /ie/, and /ue/ can be spelled with *vowel-consonant-e.* For example, in the word *cape,* the /ay/ is spelled with *a-consonant-e.* After segmenting and recording the word *cape,* draw an arrow from the *e* to the *a* underneath the word and explain that the *e* and *a* work together to spell the sound /ay/.

Lesson 3.4: Reinforcement Games for Vowel Digraphs

Materials

- multiple sets of word cards for vowel digraphs for the sound being taught; find reproducible masters for these between pages 148 and 187

- spelling-sounds sorting mat (one per group); find a reproducible master for this on page 188

- additional materials, as described in chapter 3, related to the games listed in this lesson

Instructions

Have students play games in pairs or small groups. Provide students with an opportunity to develop and consolidate their skills by using word cards for the new sound to play one of the following games:

- go fishing for sounds (see page 44)

- sound concentration (see page 44)

- beat the clock (see page 47)

- tic-tac-toe (see page 47)

- what's in the middle? (see page 45)

- sound-sorting game

To set up the sound-sorting game, have students use a spelling-sounds sorting mat to sort word cards according to the way the sound is spelled. Have students work in pairs, each taking a turn asking another student to segment words, reading the words, and placing them in the correct columns.

Extension

Place the games at a literacy center so that students may play them during free-choice activity time.

Lesson 3.5: Spelling Practice for Vowel Digraphs

Materials

- spelling-sounds sorting mats with heading labeled according to the three spellings of the sound being taught (one map per student); find a reproducible master for the sorting mat on page 188

- word cards for the vowel digraphs being taught (for teacher reference only); find reproducible masters for these between pages 148 and 187

Instructions

Give your students a spelling "test," which could be used as an actual test to assess students' mastery of the new sound. Sort word cards into separate piles according to the way the vowel digraph is spelled. From the first pile, select a word and dictate it. For example:

Teacher	The first four words in your spelling test contain the sound /er/, spelled with the letters *er*. The first word is *her*. Say each sound in the word and spell it under the heading *er*. (The students record the word *her* in the appropriate column.)

Continue with the remaining words in which the sound /er/ is spelled with the letters *er*.)

Teacher	The next three words in your spelling test contain the sound /er/, spelled with the letters *ur*. The first word is *fur*. Say each sound in the word and spell it under the heading /ur/. (The students record the word under the appropriate column.)

Continue with the remaining words in which the sound /er/ is spelled with the letters *ur*. Repeat the procedure for words in which the sound /er/ is spelled with the letters *ir*.

This lesson can also be used to assess students' mastery of the new sound and to assess students' encoding and decoding skills before moving on to a new sound. Once students have practiced spelling the words on the spelling-sounds sorting mat, have each student read the words back to you.

Lesson 3.6: Building Fluency for the Vowel Digraphs

Materials

- a variety of reading materials including fiction, nonfiction, poems, songs, readers' theater scripts, graphic novels

- bins for organizing and storing texts

Instructions

Have students practice reading and rereading texts at their independent levels. (For additional activities designed to promote reading fluency, see Rasinski.)

In order to assess their ability to use decoding skills in the context of reading authentic texts, you might wish to ask individual students to read aloud to you. Such an assessment could also indicate whether students need additional instruction and practice in specific spelling patterns.

PHONEMIC AWARENESS ASSESSMENT

The Phonemic Awareness Assessment is composed of two parts: a blending section and a segmenting section. It is intended to be administered to students on an individual basis and may not be appropriate for use with young students who have difficulty with the concept of a *nonsense word*.

When administering the assessment, do not allow the student to see the words. Sit in a quiet area, facing the student. Be sure that the student can hear you clearly and see your mouth.

Prior to administering each part of the assessment, state the instructions and provide several practice items. Be sure that the child understands the task before administering the test items. Accept the students' first response as correct or incorrect. If a student misses five consecutive items, discontinue that part of the assessment.

INSTRUCTIONS FOR PART 1: BLENDING

When administering the practice and test items, articulate each sound distinctly, leaving a one-second interval between each sound. If the student responds correctly, place a checkmark on the corresponding line. If the response is incorrect, record the student's response.

To practise, say to the student, "I'm going to say some sounds that make up a nonsense word, then I'm going to say the word. The sounds are /a/-/p/:ap. Now you try one. I'll say the sounds, and you say the word. Remember, these are not real words. /a/-/p/." The student responds, "ap."

ADDITIONAL PRACTICE ITEMS	CORRECT RESPONSE
/o/-/g/	og
/u/-/f/	uff

Students with well-developed blending skills should score above 90 percent on this part of the assessment. Students who score below 90 percent may benefit from additional instruction in this area.

Name _____   Date _____

RECORDING SHEET FOR PART 1: BLENDING

Test Items	Student Response	Correct Response
1. /r/-/ee/	_____	ree
2. /e/-/k/	_____	eck
3. /l/-/i/-/g/	_____	lig
4. /p/-/a/-/b/	_____	pab
5. /s/-/m/-/ie/	_____	smy
6. /g/-/l/-/o/-/g/	_____	glog
7. /t/-/u/-/s/-/p/	_____	tusp
8. /d/-/a/-/c/-/t/	_____	dact
9. /c/-/l/-/or/-/s/	_____	clors
10. /f/-/r/-/i/-/m/-/p/	_____	frimp
11. /b/-/l/-/ee/-/n/-/d/	_____	bleend
12. /s/-/t/-/r/-/oo/-/ck/	_____	strook

Student's score _____ divided by 12 = _____ x 100 = _____%

INSTRUCTIONS FOR PART 2: SEGMENTING

When administering the practice and test items, pronounce each nonsense word distinctly. Request that the student repeat the nonsense word before segmenting it. If necessary, correct the student's pronunciation before allowing the student to segment the word. Instruct the student to leave a one-second "space" between each sound. For each sound (phoneme) that the student correctly segments, place a checkmark on the corresponding line. If a student partially segments a word, give checkmarks only for those phonemes that are articulated individually. (For example, if a student segments the nonsense word *spim* as /sp-/i/-/m/, only the final two phonemes would be scored as correct.)

To practise, say to the student, "I'm going to say a nonsense word, then I'm going to say each sound in that word. The word is *ip*: /i/-/p/. Now you try it. Say *ip*, then say each sound in the word *ip*." The student responds, "ip: /i/-/p/."

ADDITIONAL PRACTICE ITEMS	CORRECT RESPONSE
ibe	/ie/-/b/
ork	/or/-/k/

Students with well-developed segmenting skills should score above 90 percent on this part of the assessment. Students who score below 90 percent may benefit from additional instruction in this area.

Both parts of this assessment begin with simple items (VC and CVC words) and progress to more complex tasks (CCVC, CVCC, CCVCC, CCCVC words). Although raw scores can be calculated, we recommend that you pay closer attention to the *types* of errors that the student makes. Many students can blend and segment simple VC or CVC words but experience difficulty with the adjacent consonant sounds in CCVC, CVCC, or CCCVCC words. Other students may be successful at blending but have difficulty segmenting. Testing data can assist you in planning instruction that will address the needs of individual students.

Name _____ Date _____

RECORDING SHEET FOR PART 2: SEGMENTING

TEST ITEMS	STUDENT RESPONSE	CORRECT RESPONSE
1. ep	___ - ___	/e/-/p/
2. tay	___ - ___	/t/-/ay/
3. lat	___ - ___ - ___	/l/-/a/-/t/
4. jick	___ - ___ - ___	/j/-/i/-/ck/
5. spip	___ - ___ - ___ - ___	/s/-/p/-/i/-/p/
6. drot	___ - ___ - ___ - ___	/d/-/r/-/o/-/t/
7. bisp	___ - ___ - ___ - ___	/b/-/i/-/s/-/p/
8. hant	___ - ___ - ___ - ___	/h/-/a/-/n/-/t/
9. ployd	___ - ___ - ___ - ___	/p/-/l/-/oy/-/d/
10. grost	___ - ___ - ___ - ___ - ___	/g/-/r/-/o/-/s/-/t/
11. clind	___ - ___ - ___ - ___ - ___	/c/-/l/-/i/-/n/-/d/
12. strump	___ - ___ - ___ - ___ - ___ - ___	/s/-/t/-/r/-/u/-/m/-/p/

Student's score _____ divided by 46 = _____ x 100 = _____%

ALPHABETIC CODING ASSESSMENT
Instructions to the Teacher

The Alphabetic Coding Assessment is intended to be administered to students individually. Provide the student with the student copy of the assessment. Say to the student, "I'm going to show you some letters, and I want you to tell me the sounds that the letters spell. If you don't know the answer, don't guess. Just say 'pass'."

Point to the first item in part 1. Ask the student, "What sound does this letter spell?" Allow the student no more than three seconds to respond before moving on to the next item. If the student does not respond within the three-second time limit, score the item as incorrect. If the student responds with the name of a letter, reply, "Yes, that's the *name* of the letter, but what *sound* does it spell?" Indicate correct responses on the recording sheet with a checkmark on the corresponding line. If the student responds incorrectly, you may wish to record the incorrect response on the line provided. For your reference only, key words are provided on the examiner's copy to indicate correct responses.

If a student demonstrates strong familiarity with part 1 of the assessment, proceed to part 2, and so on. Or, you may choose to administer only the section(s) of the assessment that is an area of concern. If a student misses five consecutive items, it may be advisable to discontinue the assessment. Note that this assessment is not intended to include the entire alphabetic code. Rather, it is intended to provide examiners with information relating to a student's knowledge of common spelling patterns (graphemes). (A grapheme is a letter or group of letters that spell a single sound.)

SCORING

A response is scored as correct only if the student correctly identifies an individual sound that is represented by the letter(s). If the student responds with a word containing that sound, the response is scored as incorrect. This assessment provides valuable information about a student's ability to recognize graphemes. We recommend that, instead of calculating a raw score, you use this assessment to determine the letters and letters combinations that the student cannot yet identify. This information can then be used to plan appropriate instructional interventions.

ALPHABETIC CODING ASSESSMENT
Student Copy

PART 1: CONSONANTS

d   h   l   p   s   w   z   b   f   j

m   r   v   y   c   g   k   n   t   x

PART 2: SHORT-VOWEL SOUNDS

a   e   i   o   u

PART 3: CONSONANT DIGRAPHS

ck   sh   ch   th   qu   wr   kn   ph   tch

wh   gh

PART 4: VOWEL DIGRAPHS

or   er   ea   ir   oa   ur   ee   ie   ay

ey   ou   ai   oi   ow   oy   oo   oe   au

ew   aw   ui   igh   ough   augh   eigh

Alphabetic Coding Assessment (page 2)

ALPHABETIC CODING ASSESSMENT
Teacher Recording Sheet

PART 1: CONSONANTS

Although some letters are used to represent more than one sound (for example the letter *g* can spell /g/, as in *girl*; or /j/, as in *giraffe*), this section is intended to determine whether students can identify the most common sound-symbol correspondences. For your reference only, key words are noted next to the item to indicate the correct response. Provide each student with his or her own Alphabetic Coding Assessment copy (page 112). While pointing to the first item in part 1, ask the student, "What sound does this letter spell?" The student responds, "/d/".

d ___ (**d**og)   h ___ (**h**at)   l ___ (**l**ike)   p ___ (**p**ie)   s ___ (**s**ip)   w ___ (**w**in)

z ___ (**z**oo)   b ___ (**b**oy)   f ___ (**f**ar)   j ___ (**j**am)   m ___ (**m**an)   r ___ (**r**an)*

v ___ (**v**an)   y ___ (**y**am)   c ___ (**c**at)   g ___ (**g**irl)   k ___ (**k**ing)   n ___ (**n**ew)

t ___ (**t**all)   x ___ (a**x**)**

* /er/ is not an acceptable response for the letter *r*.
** Technically, the letter *x* does not represent a simple one-to-one mapping pattern, since it is a single-letter symbol that is used to represent two phonemes: /k/ and /s/. However, as this does not present problems for students with respect to reading, we have chosen to treat *x* as a simple sound.

PART 2: SHORT VOWEL SOUNDS

This section is intended to assess the student's ability to identify short vowel sounds. If the student responds with a long vowel sound (which is also the letter name), instruct the student to provide you with the sound that the letter usually spells (the short vowel sound). While pointing to the first item in part 2, ask the student, "What sound does this letter spell?" The student responds, "/a/" as in *cat*.

a ___ (c**a**p)   e ___ (g**e**t)   i ___ (b**i**t)   o ___ (p**o**t)   u ___ (c**u**p)

(Teacher Recording Sheet continued)

PART 3: CONSONANT DIGRAPHS

While pointing to the first item in part 3, ask the student, "What sound does this letter spell?" The student responds, "/ck/".

ck ___ (pa**ck**)   sh ___ (**sh**op)   ch ___ (**ch**ip)

th ___ (**th**in; **th**en)*   qu ___ (**qu**it)   wr ___ (/r/ as in **wr**ite)

kn ___ (/n/ as in **kn**ow) ph ___ (/f/ as in tele**ph**one) tch ___ (/ch/ as in ca**tch**)

wh ___ (**wh**ich)   gh ___ (/g/ as in **gh**ost; or /f/ as in cou**gh**)

*The letters *th* are commonly used to spell two different sounds: /th/ as in *thin*, and /th/ as in *then*. Either response is correct. You may wish to circle the corresponding key word to indicate the student's response.

PART 4: VOWEL DIGRAPHS

This section is intended to assess the student's ability to identify complex mapping patterns. Many of these graphemes (spelling patterns) are used to spell more than one sound. When appropriate, more than one correct response is indicated. Students need provide only one correct response, which the examiner can note by circling the corresponding key word.

In some (rare) instances, a student may provide an alternate response that could be scored as correct. If the student responds with a phoneme that is not listed next to the digraph, ask the student to give you an example of a word that contains that sound or spelling pattern. For example if a student stated that the letters *ou* spelled the sound /oa/, and was able to provide the word *soul* as an example, the response would be scored as correct. If the student was unable to provide an appropriate example, the response would be scored as incorrect. While pointing to the first item in part 4, ask the student, "What sound does this letter spell?" The student responds, "/or/".

or ___ (/or/ as in **f**or**k**; /er/ as in **wor**k)

er ___ (/er/ as in **ver**b)

ea ___ (/ee/ as in m**ea**t; /e/ as in br**ea**d; /ay/ as in gr**ea**t)

ir ___ (/er/ as in **fir**)

oa ___ (/oa/ as in c**oa**t)

Alphabetic Coding Assessment (page 4)

(Teacher Recording Sheet continued)

ur   ___ (/er/ as in f**ur**)

ee   ___ (/ee/ as in m**ee**t)

ie   ___ (/ie/ as in p**ie**; /ee/ as in th**ie**f)

ay   ___ (/ay/ as in d**ay**)

ey   ___ (/ee/ as in monk**ey**; /ay/ as in th**ey**)

ou   ___ (/ow/ as in c**ou**ch; /u/ as in t**ou**ch; /oo/ as in tr**ou**pe)

ai   ___ (/ay/ as in p**ai**d; /e/ as in s**ai**d)

oi   ___ (/oy/ as in **oi**l)

ow   ___ (/ow/ as in c**ow**; /oa/ as in sn**ow**)

oy   ___ (/oy/ as in t**oy**)

oo   ___ (/oo/ as in s**oo**n; /oo/ as in l**oo**k)

oe   ___ (/oa/ as in d**oe**; /oo/ as in sh**oe**)

au   ___ (/o/ as in **Au**gust)

ew   ___ (/oo/ as in cr**ew**; /ue/ as in c**ue**)

aw   ___ (/o/ as in p**aw**)

ui   ___ (/oo/ as in r**ui**n)

igh   ___ (/ie/ as in s**igh**)

ough ___ (/o/ as in th**ough**t; /oo/ as in thr**ough**; /oa/ as in thor**ough**)

augh ___ (/o/ as in t**augh**t)

eigh ___ (/ay/ as in **eigh**t)

ORDER FOR TEACHING THE SIMPLE SOUNDS

SOUND GROUP *A* WORD LIST: /s/, /a/ (as in *cat*), /t/, /p/, /h/, /i/ (as in *pin*), /n/

at	an	sat	sap	sip
pat	pit	pin	tap	tan
tip	tin	hat	hit	hip
nip	nap	past	hint	snap
snip	spit	spin		

Words for lesson 1.3 (in this order): sat, hat, hit, pit, pin, tin, tan, tap, tip, hip

SOUND GROUP *B* WORD LIST: /b/, /o/ (as in *hot*), /m/, /r/, /c/ (as in *cat*)

on	rot	cab	map	ran
man	bit	mob	bib	bob
mop	hot	Ron	rob	pot
cot	hop	rip	rat	spot
ramp	cram	crib	brat	scrap
stop	cramp	stomp	stamp	camp

Words for lesson 1.3 (in this order): pot, rot, rat, ran, man, map, mop, mob, bob, bib

SOUND GROUP *C* WORD LIST: /d/, /e/ (as in *bet*), /l/, /g/ (as in *go*)

get	red	sad	hid	lid
got	big	bad	log	leg
dip	let	dog	bed	lot
grip	brag	slob	grim	plop
glad	help	slap	stem	sled
slip	grasp	strap	brand	print

Words for lesson 1.3 (in this order): red, bed, bet, get, let, leg, log, dog, dig, big

For Lessons 1.1 to 1.7

SOUND GROUP *D* WORD LIST: /f/, /u/ (as in *fun*), /j/, /y/ (as in *yet*)

fun	yet	us	jet	yes
fog	up	fin	jug	jog
run	jab	fit	ram	flag
flip	fast	frog	glum	slug
jump	yelp	gulp	drum	gum
rut	Gus	just	flat	flint
fact	fund	film	plug	plum

Words for lesson 1.3 (in this order): flag, flap, flip, flit, slit, slip, slap, slam, clam, cram, crab

SOUND GROUP *E* WORD LIST: /v/, /w/, /x/, /z/

ax	zip	six	Oz	fax
zig	zag	wet	wit	vet
van	web	fox	wax	box
yam	yak	wig	zap	tax
vest	rest	wind	exit	west
twig	vent	wept	wisp	welt

Words for lesson 1.3 (in this order): vest, vent, sent, went, west, welt, wilt

Name _____ Date _____

PHONEMIC AWARENESS AND ALPHABETIC CODING ASSESSMENTS FOR SOUND GROUP *A*

Teacher Recording Sheet

ALPHABETIC CODE KNOWLEDGE

On the student recording sheet, point to each letter-symbol individually. Ask the student, "What sound does this letter spell?" Circle each correct response below:

s   a   t   p   h   i   n

Score _____ divided by 7 = _____ x 100 = _____%

PHONEMIC AWARENESS: BLENDING

Say to the student, "I'm going to say the sounds in a word, and I want you to tell me the word." Sit in a way that the student can hear you clearly and see your mouth. Say each sound in the following words distinctly, allowing a one-second interval between each sound. Do not allow the student to see the words. Record the student's first response as correct (✓) or incorrect (X).

/a/-/t/ _____   /h/-/a/-/t/ _____   /s/-/i/-/p/ _____   /i/-/n/ _____

/s/-/i/-/t/ _____   /n/-/a/-/p/ _____   /p/-/a/-/s/-/t/ _____

/s/-/n/-/i/-/p/ _____   /h/-/i/-/n/-/t/ _____   /n/-/i/-/p/-/s/ _____

Score _____ divided by 10 = _____ x 100 = _____%

PHONEMIC AWARENESS: SEGMENTING

Say to the student, "I'm going to say a word. I want you to repeat the word then tell me each of the sounds in that word." Sit in a way that the student can hear you clearly and see your mouth but cannot see the words on your sheet. Pronounce each word distinctly. Do not allow the student to see the words.

it _____   an _____   nip _____   tin _____

pit _____   spit _____   hint _____   pins _____

snap _____   taps _____

Score _____ divided by 10 = _____ x 100 = _____%

Assessments for Sound Group *A* (page 1)

(Teacher Recording Sheet continued)

DECODING

Ask the student to read each of the following words for student recording sheet:

it _____   in _____   nip _____   pit _____

nap _____   pin _____   hit _____   tap _____

pins _____   spin _____   hint _____   sits _____

Score _____ divided by 12 = _____ x 100 = _____%

ENCODING

Ask the student to spell each of the following words on the student recording sheet:

at _____   sip _____   pan _____   sit _____

tan _____   pan _____   sips _____   past _____

hint _____   spat _____   taps _____   snap _____

Score _____ divided by 12 = _____ x 100 = _____%

CALCULATING OVERALL SCORE

Blending _____   Segmenting _____

Decoding _____   Encoding _____

Total score _____ divided by 51 = _____ x 100 = _____%

Student Recording Sheet

ALPHABETIC CODE KNOWLEDGE

s   a   t   p   h   i   n

DECODING

it   in   nip   pit

nap   pin   hit   tap

pins   spin   hint   sits

ENCODING

_____   _____   _____

_____   _____   _____

_____   _____   _____

Assessments for Sound Group A (page 3)

Name _____   Date _____

PHONEMIC AWARENESS AND ALPHABETIC CODING ASSESSMENTS FOR SOUND GROUP *B*
Teacher Recording Sheet

ALPHABETIC CODE KNOWLEDGE

On the student recording sheet, point to each letter-symbol individually. Ask the student, "What sound does this letter spell?" Circle each correct response below:

b   o   m   r   c

Score _____ divided by 5 = _____ x 100 = _____%

PHONEMIC AWARENESS: BLENDING

Say to the student, "I'm going to say the sounds in a word, and I want you to tell me the word." Sit in a way that the student can hear you clearly and see your mouth. Say each sound in the following words distinctly, allowing a one-second interval between each sound. Record the student's first response as correct (✓) or incorrect (X).

/c/-/o/-/t/ _____   /r/-/i/-/p/ _____   /c/-/a/-/b/ _____   /m/-/a/-/p/ _____

/r/-/a/-/n/ _____   /b/-/i/-/t/ _____   /h/-/o/-/p/ _____   /b/-/r/-/a/-/t/ _____

/s/-/t/-/o/-/m/-/p/ _____   /r/-/a/-/m/-/p/ _____

Score _____ divided by 10 = _____ x 100 = _____%

PHONEMIC AWARENESS: SEGMENTING

Say to the student, "I'm going to say a word. I want you to repeat the word then tell me each of the sounds in that word." Sit in a way that the student can hear you clearly and see your mouth but cannot see the words on your sheet. Pronounce each word distinctly.

on _____   man _____   cot _____   rob _____

cram _____   brim _____   stop _____   stamp _____

scrap _____   cramp _____

Score _____ divided by 10 = _____ x 100 = _____%

Name _____   Date _____

DECODING

Ask the student to read each of the following words from the student recording sheet:

mop _____   hot _____   bib _____   pop _____

rat _____   ran _____   Ron _____   spot _____

crib _____   cram _____   stomp _____   scrap _____

Score _____ divided by 12 = _____ x 100 = _____%

ENCODING

Ask the student to spell each of the following words on the student recording sheet:

on _____   map _____   bit _____   pot _____

rob _____   rip _____   hot _____   brat _____

ramp _____   cramp _____   strap _____   stamp _____

Score _____ divided by 12 = _____ x 100 = _____%

CALCULATING OVERALL SCORE

Blending _____   Segmenting _____

Decoding _____   Encoding _____

Total score _____ divided by 49 = _____ x 100 = _____%

Student Recording Sheet

ALPHABETIC CODE KNOWLEDGE

b   o   m   r   c

DECODING

mop	hot	bib	pop
rat	ran	Ron	spot
crib	cram	stomp	scrap

ENCODING

_____   _____   _____

_____   _____   _____

_____   _____   _____

_____   _____   _____

Name _____   Date _____

PHONEMIC AWARENESS AND ALPHABETIC CODING ASSESSMENTS FOR SOUND GROUP *C*
Teacher Recording Sheet

ALPHABETIC CODE KNOWLEDGE

On the student recording sheet, point to each letter-symbol individually. Ask the student, "What sound does this letter spell?" Circle each correct response below:

d   e   l   g

Score _____ divided by 4 = _____ x 100 = _____%

PHONEMIC AWARENESS: BLENDING

Say to the student, "I'm going to say the sounds in a word, and I want you to tell me the word." Sit in a way that the student can hear you clearly and see your mouth. Say each sound in the following words distinctly, allowing a one-second interval between each sound. Record the student's first response as correct (✓) or incorrect (X).

/g/-/o/-/t/ _____   /r/-/e/-/d/ _____   /s/-/a/-/d/ _____   /l/-/i/-/d/ _____

/l/-/e/-/t/ _____   /d/-/o/-/g/ _____   /s/-/l/-/o/-/p/ _____

/g/-/l/-/a/-/d/ _____   /s/-/l/-/e/-/d/ _____   /g/-/r/-/a/-/s/-/p/ _____

Score _____ divided by 10 = _____ x 100 = _____%

PHONEMIC AWARENESS: SEGMENTING

Say to the student, "I'm going to say a word. I want you to repeat the word then tell me each of the sounds in that word." Sit in a way that the student can hear you clearly and see your mouth but cannot see the words on your sheet. Pronounce each word distinctly.

get _____   dip _____   log _____   bed _____

bad _____   big _____   leg _____   grip _____

drop _____   spend _____

Score _____ divided by 10 = _____ x 100 = _____%

Assessments for Sound Group *C* (page 1)

Name _____   Date _____

(Teacher Recording Sheet continued)

DECODING

Ask the student to read each of the following words from the student recording sheet:

bed _____   lot _____   get _____   big _____

dog _____   dip _____   slob _____   stem _____

help _____   plop _____   brand _____   slap _____

Score _____ divided by 12 = _____ x 100 = _____%

ENCODING

Ask the student to spell each of the following words on the student recording sheet:

red _____   lid _____   got _____   bad _____

leg _____   log _____   let _____   hid _____

grip _____   brag _____   sled _____   stem _____

Score _____ divided by 12 = _____ x 100 = _____%

CALCULATING OVERALL SCORE

Blending _____   Segmenting _____

Decoding _____   Encoding _____

Total score _____ divided by 48 = _____ x 100 = _____

Student Recording Sheet

ALPHABETIC CODE KNOWLEDGE

d   e   l   g

DECODING

bed	lot	get	big
dog	dip	slob	stem
help	plop	brand	slap

ENCODING

_____   _____   _____

_____   _____   _____

_____   _____   _____

Assessments for Sound Group C (page 3)

Name _____   Date _____

PHONEMIC AWARENESS AND ALPHABETIC CODING ASSESSMENTS FOR SOUND GROUP *D*

Teacher Recording Sheet

ALPHABETIC CODE KNOWLEDGE

On the student recording sheet, point to each letter-symbol individually. Ask the student, "What sound does this letter spell?" Circle each correct response below:

f   u   j   y

Score _____ divided by 4 = _____ x 100 = _____%

PHONEMIC AWARENESS: BLENDING

Say to the student, "I'm going to say the sounds in a word, and I want you to tell me the word." Sit in a way that the student can hear you clearly and see your mouth. Say each sound in the following words distinctly, allowing a one-second interval between each sound. Record the student's first response as correct (✓) or incorrect (X).

/f/-/u/-/n/ _____   /y/-/e/-/t/ _____   /j/-/u/-/g/ _____   /j/-/o/-/g/ _____

/j/-/a/-/b/ _____   /f/-/i/-/t/ _____   /y/-/e/-/l/-/p/ _____

/d/-/r/-/u/-/m/ _____   /f/-/i/-/l/-/m/ _____   /f/-/l/-/i/-/n/-/t/ _____

Score _____ divided by 10 = _____ x 100 = _____%

PHONEMIC AWARENESS: SEGMENTING

Say to the student, "I'm going to say a word. I want you to repeat the word then tell me each of the sounds in that word." Sit in a way that the student can hear you clearly and see your mouth but cannot see the words on your sheet. Pronounce each word distinctly.

us _____   up _____   jet _____   yes _____

fog _____   fin _____   run _____   flag _____

glum _____   glint _____

Score _____ divided by 10 = _____ x 100 = _____%

Name _____   Date _____

(Teacher Recording Sheet continued)

DECODING

Ask the student to read each of the following words from the student recording sheet:

fog _____   fin _____   jog _____   jug _____

run _____   flip _____   fast _____   slug _____

gulp _____   just _____   fact _____   stump _____

Score _____ divided by 12 = _____ x 100 = _____%

ENCODING

Ask the student to spell each of the following words on the student recording sheet:

fun _____   yet _____   gum _____   jut _____

fit _____   yes _____   flat _____   frog _____

drum _____   jump _____   film _____   plug _____

Score _____ divided by 12 = _____ x 100 = _____%

CALCULATING OVERALL SCORE

Blending _____   Segmenting _____

Decoding _____   Encoding _____

Total score _____ divided by 48 = _____ x 100 = _____%

Assessments for Sound Group *D* (page 2)

Name _____ Date _____

Student Recording Sheet

ALPHABETIC CODE KNOWLEDGE

f   u   j   y

DECODING

fog	fin	jog	jug
run	flip	fast	slug
gulp	just	fact	stump

ENCODING

_____ _____ _____

_____ _____ _____

_____ _____ _____

_____ _____ _____

Name _____   Date _____

PHONEMIC AWARENESS AND ALPHABETIC CODING ASSESSMENTS FOR SOUND GROUP *E*

Teacher Recording Sheet

ALPHABETIC CODE KNOWLEDGE

On the student recording sheet, point to each letter-symbol individually. Ask the student, "What sound does this letter spell?" Circle each correct response below:

v   w   x   z

Score _____ divided by 4 = _____ x 100 = _____%

PHONEMIC AWARENESS: BLENDING

Say to the student, "I'm going to say the sounds in a word, and I want you to tell me the word." Sit in a way that the student can hear you clearly and see your mouth. Say each sound in the following words distinctly, allowing a one-second interval between each sound. Record the student's first response as correct (✓) or incorrect (X).

/f/-/o/-/x/ _____   /z/-/i/-/p/ _____   /t/-/a/-/x/ _____   /z/-/i/-/g/ _____

/w/-/a/-/x/ _____   /b/-/o/-/x/ _____   /v/-/e/-/n/-/t/ _____

/w/-/i/-/n/-/d/ _____   /e/-/x/-/i/-/t/ _____   /w/-/e/-/l/-/t/ _____

Score _____ divided by 10 = _____ x 100 = _____%

PHONEMIC AWARENESS: SEGMENTING

Say to the student, "I'm going to say a word. I want you to repeat the word then tell me each of the sounds in that word." Sit in a way that the student can hear you clearly and see your mouth but cannot see the words. Pronounce each word distinctly. (Note that the letter *x* represents two phonemes. For example, students can segment the word *ax* as "/a/-/x/" or /a/-/k/-/s/". Either response is acceptable.)

Oz _____   ax _____   six _____   yam _____   fax _____

vest _____   wept _____   twig _____   wisp _____   welt_____

Score _____ divided by 10 = _____ x 100 = _____%

Assessments for Sound Group *E* (page 1)

(Teacher Recording Sheet continued)

DECODING

Ask the student to read each of the following words from the student recording sheet:

zip _____   zap _____   six _____   fax _____

van _____   wig _____   swept _____   crept_____

wind _____   wisp _____   went _____   swift_____

Score _____ divided by 12 = _____ x 100 = _____%

ENCODING

Ask the student to spell each of the following words on the student recording sheet:

ax _____   Oz _____   zig _____   zag _____

wet _____   wit _____   web _____   vet_____

fox _____   twig_____   west _____   wept _____

Score _____ divided by 12 = _____ x 100 = _____%

CALCULATING OVERALL SCORE

Blending _____   Segmenting _____

Decoding _____   Encoding _____

Total score _____ divided by 48 = _____ x 100 = _____%

Student Recording Sheet

ALPHABETIC CODE KNOWLEDGE

v   w   x   z

DECODING

zip	zap	six	fax
van	wig	swept	crept
wind	wisp	went	swift

ENCODING

_____   _____   _____

_____   _____   _____

_____   _____   _____

_____   _____   _____

Name _____   Date _____

ASSESSMENT FOR CONSONANT DIGRAPHS
Teacher Recording Sheet

Note: This assessment may be completed after /sh/, /th/, /ch/, and /ck/ have been taught.

DECODING

Ask the student to read each of the following words from the student recording sheet:

fish _____	much _____	math _____	duck _____
shelf _____	chest _____	then _____	crash_____
track _____	thick _____		

Score _____ divided by 10 = _____ x 100 = _____%

ENCODING

Ask the student to spell each of the following words on the student recording sheet:

rash _____	chip _____	path _____	pack_____
this_____	brick _____	cloth _____	shift _____
branch _____	thump_____		

Score _____ divided by 10 = _____ x 100 = _____%

CALCULATING OVERALL SCORE

Total of both scores _____ divided by 20 = _____ x 100 = _____%

Student Recording Sheet

DECODING

fish	much	math	duck
chest	then	crash	shelf
track	thick		

ENCODING

_____   _____   _____

_____   _____   _____

_____   _____   _____

_____

Assessment for Consonant Digraphs (page 2)

SPELLING-THE-SOUND SHEET

The Consonant Digraph *sh*

ship   _____ _____ _____

shot   _____ _____ _____

shut   _____ _____ _____

cash   _____ _____ _____

rash   _____ _____ _____

fish   _____ _____ _____

shop   _____ _____ _____

wish   _____ _____ _____

crash   _____ _____ _____ _____

shelf   _____ _____ _____ _____

shaft   _____ _____ _____ _____

shift   _____ _____ _____ _____

WORD CARDS FOR CONSONANT DIGRAPHS

SPELLING THE SOUND /sh/

ship	shot
shut	cash
rash	fish
wish	crash

WORD CARDS FOR CONSONANT DIGRAPHS

SPELLING THE SOUND /sh/

shelf	shaft
shin	shop
sash	dish
gash	shift

SPELLING-THE-SOUND SHEET

The Consonant Digraph *ch*

much   _____ _____ _____

chop   _____ _____ _____

chat   _____ _____ _____

chip   _____ _____ _____

chin   _____ _____ _____

chest   _____ _____ _____ _____

bunch   _____ _____ _____ _____

lunch   _____ _____ _____ _____

pinch   _____ _____ _____ _____

chimp   _____ _____ _____ _____

branch   _____ _____ _____ _____ _____

brunch   _____ _____ _____ _____ _____

WORD CARDS FOR CONSONANT DIGRAPHS

SPELLING THE SOUND /ch/

much	chop
chat	chip
chin	chest
bunch	lunch

WORD CARDS FOR CONSONANT DIGRAPHS

SPELLING THE SOUND /ch/

pinch	branch
chap	champ
chimp	munch
hunch	brunch

Name _____   Date _____

SPELLING-THE-SOUND SHEET
The Consonant Digraph *th*

bath   _____ _____ _____

math   _____ _____ _____

path   _____ _____ _____

with   _____ _____ _____

thin   _____ _____ _____

that   _____ _____ _____

then   _____ _____ _____

cloth   _____ _____ _____ _____

filth   _____ _____ _____ _____

thump   _____ _____ _____ _____

month   _____ _____ _____ _____

thrust   _____ _____ _____ _____ _____

WORD CARDS FOR CONSONANT DIGRAPHS

SPELLING THE SOUND /th/

bath	math
path	with
thin	that
then	cloth

WORD CARDS FOR CONSONANT DIGRAPHS

SPELLING THE SOUND /th/

thump	thrust
moth	this
month	throb
sloth	filth

SPELLING-THE-SOUND SHEET
The Consonant Digraph *ck*

pick   _____   _____   _____

duck   _____   _____   _____

sock   _____   _____   _____

pack   _____   _____   _____

luck   _____   _____   _____

stick   _____   _____   _____   _____

black   _____   _____   _____   _____

stuck   _____   _____   _____   _____

track   _____   _____   _____   _____

brick   _____   _____   _____   _____

truck   _____   _____   _____   _____

clock   _____   _____   _____   _____

WORD CARDS FOR CONSONANT DIGRAPHS

SPELLING THE SOUND /ck/

pick	duck
clock	pack
luck	stick
black	stuck

WORD CARDS FOR CONSONANT DIGRAPHS

SPELLING THE SOUND /ck/

track	brick
truck	sock
lock	clock
muck	slick

SPELLING-THE-SOUND SHEET
The Vowel Digraph /er/ with *er, ir, ur*

her   _____ _____

sir   _____ _____

fur   _____ _____

hurt   _____ _____ _____

bird   _____ _____ _____

third   _____ _____ _____

under   _____ _____ _____ _____

after   _____ _____ _____ _____

burst   _____ _____ _____ _____

thirst   _____ _____ _____ _____

enter   _____ _____ _____ _____

swirl   _____ _____ _____ _____

WORD CARDS FOR THE VOWEL DIGRAPHS

SPELLING THE SOUND /er/ with *er, ir, ur*

her	sir
fur	hurt
bird	third
under	after

WORD CARDS FOR THE VOWEL DIGRAPHS

SPELLING THE SOUND /er/ with _er, ir, ur_

burst	thirst
enter	swirl
fern	turn
first	shirt

SPELLING-THE-SOUND SHEET

The Vowel Digraph /or/ with *or, ore, oor*

tore _____ _____

door _____ _____

wore _____ _____

shore _____ _____

corn _____ _____ _____

north _____ _____ _____

worn _____ _____ _____

store _____ _____ _____

floor _____ _____ _____

short _____ _____ _____

sort _____ _____ _____

snore _____ _____ _____

WORD CARDS FOR THE VOWEL DIGRAPHS

SPELLING THE SOUND /or/ with *or, ore, oor*

worn	corn
tore	wore
door	store
north	shore

WORD CARDS FOR THE VOWEL DIGRAPHS

SPELLING THE SOUND /or/ with *or, ore, oor*

floor	short
sort	snort
more	torn
score	horn

SPELLING-THE-SOUND SHEET

The Vowel Digraph /ar/ with *ar, are*

are   _____

jar   _____   _____

art   _____   _____

card   _____   _____   _____

part   _____   _____   _____

barn   _____   _____   _____

yard   _____   _____   _____

charm   _____   _____   _____

star   _____   _____   _____

scar   _____   _____   _____

start   _____   _____   _____   _____

snarl   _____   _____   _____   _____

WORD CARDS FOR THE VOWEL DIGRAPHS

SPELLING THE SOUND /ar/ with *ar, are*

are	jar
art	card
part	barn
yard	charm

WORD CARDS FOR THE VOWEL DIGRAPHS

SPELLING THE SOUND /ar/ with *ar, are*

star	scar
start	snarl
farm	scarf
alarm	aren't

SPELLING-THE-SOUND SHEET

The Vowel Digraph /ay/ with *a–consonant–e, ai, ay*

say   _____ _____

may   _____ _____

pay   _____ _____

cape   _____ _____ _____ e

rain   _____ _____ _____

play   _____ _____ _____

sail   _____ _____ _____

made   _____ _____ _____ e

late   _____ _____ _____ e

wait   _____ _____ _____

name   _____ _____ _____ e

snail _____ _____ _____ _____

WORD CARDS FOR THE VOWEL DIGRAPHS

SPELLING THE SOUND /ay/ with *a–consonant–e, ai, ay*

cape	rain
pay	play
sail	made
late	may

WORD CARDS FOR THE VOWEL DIGRAPHS

SPELLING THE SOUND /ay/ with *a–consonant–e, ai, ay*

snail	wait
say	name
clay	tray
Jane	afraid

SPELLING-THE-SOUND SHEET

The Vowel Digraph /ee/ with *ee, ea, ie*

see   _____ _____

leaf   _____ _____ _____

beat   _____ _____ _____

feet   _____ _____ _____

meat   _____ _____ _____

thief   _____ _____ _____

real   _____ _____ _____

beach   _____ _____ _____

green   _____ _____ _____ _____

field   _____ _____ _____ _____

sleep   _____ _____ _____ _____

sweet   _____ _____ _____ _____

WORD CARDS FOR THE VOWEL DIGRAPHS

SPELLING THE SOUND /ee/ with *ee, ea, ie*

see	leaf
beat	feet
meat	thief
real	beach

WORD CARDS FOR THE VOWEL DIGRAPHS

SPELLING THE SOUND /ee/ with *ee, ea, ie*

green	field
sleep	sweet
reach	peach
street	greet

SPELLING-THE-SOUND SHEET

The Vowel Digraph /ie/ with *i–consonant–e, igh, y*

my   _____ _____

by   _____ _____

five   _____ _____ _____ e

fly   _____ _____ _____

right   _____ _____ _____

life   _____ _____ _____ e

ride   _____ _____ _____ e

might   _____ _____ _____

try   _____ _____ _____

fight   _____ _____ _____

slide   _____ _____ _____ _____ e

fright _____ _____ _____ _____

WORD CARDS FOR THE VOWEL DIGRAPHS

SPELLING THE SOUND /ie/ with *i–consonant–e, igh, y*

five	fly
right	my
by	life
ride	might

WORD CARDS FOR THE VOWEL DIGRAPHS

SPELLING THE SOUND /ie/ with *i–consonant–e, igh, y*

try	slide
fight	fright
lime	cry
crime	dime

SPELLING-THE-SOUND SHEET

The Vowel Digraph /oa/ with *o–consonant–e, oa, ow*

show _____ _____

home _____ _____ _____ e

boat _____ _____ _____

road _____ _____ _____

pole _____ _____ _____ e

slow _____ _____ _____

toad _____ _____ _____

blow _____ _____ _____

grow _____ _____ _____

groan _____ _____ _____ _____

close _____ _____ _____ _____ e

alone _____ _____ _____ _____ e

WORD CARDS FOR THE VOWEL DIGRAPHS

SPELLING THE SOUND /oa/ with *o–consonant–e, oa, ow*

home	boat
road	show
pole	slow
toad	blow

WORD CARDS FOR THE VOWEL DIGRAPHS

SPELLING THE SOUND /oa/ with *o–consonant–e, oa, ow*

grow	groan
close	alone
flow	glow
float	doze

SPELLING-THE-SOUND SHEET

The Vowel Digraph /ue/ with *u–consonant–e, ew, ue*

use   _____ _____e

few   _____ _____

cue   _____ _____

mew   _____ _____

fuse   _____ _____ _____e

amuse_____ _____ _____ _____e

rescue_____ _____ _____ _____ _____

refuse _____ _____ _____ _____ _____e

WORD CARDS FOR THE VOWEL DIGRAPHS

SPELLING THE SOUND /ue/ with *u–consonant–e, ew, ue*

use	mew
few	fuse
cue	amuse
rescue	refuse

SPELLING-THE-SOUND SHEET

The Vowel Digraph /oo/ with *oo, oul, u*

put   _____ _____ _____

look   _____ _____ _____

good   _____ _____ _____

wood   _____ _____ _____

shook   _____ _____ _____

cook   _____ _____ _____

book   _____ _____ _____

could   _____ _____ _____

hook   _____ _____ _____

would   _____ _____ _____

should   _____ _____ _____

stood   _____ _____ _____ _____

WORD CARDS FOR THE VOWEL DIGRAPHS

SPELLING THE SOUND /oo/ (book) with *oo, oul, u*

look	good
wood	shook
cook	book
could	hook

WORD CARDS FOR THE VOWEL DIGRAPHS

SPELLING THE SOUND /oo/ (book) with *oo, oul, u*

would	should
stood	put
brook	hood
cook	soot

SPELLING-THE-SOUND SHEET

The Vowel Digraph /ow/ with *ow, ou, ough*

cow   _____ _____

now   _____ _____

bough   _____ _____

owl   _____ _____

how   _____ _____

out   _____ _____

ouch   _____ _____

shout   _____ _____ _____

mouth   _____ _____ _____

plough   _____ _____ _____

brown   _____ _____ _____ _____

growl   _____ _____ _____ _____

WORD CARDS FOR THE VOWEL DIGRAPHS

SPELLING THE SOUND /ow/ (cow) with *ow, ou, ough*

cow	now
owl	how
out	ouch
shout	mouth

WORD CARDS FOR THE VOWEL DIGRAPHS

SPELLING THE SOUND /ow/ (cow) with *ow, ou, ough*

plough	brown
pout	growl
bough	chow
flower	power

SPELLING-THE-SOUND SHEET

The Vowel Digraph /oi/ with *oi, oy*

oil   _____ _____

boy   _____ _____

toy   _____ _____

joy   _____ _____

soil   _____ _____ _____

join   _____ _____ _____

boil   _____ _____ _____

point   _____ _____ _____ _____

moist   _____ _____ _____ _____

enjoy   _____ _____ _____ _____

spoil   _____ _____ _____ _____

oyster _____ _____ _____ _____

WORD CARDS FOR THE VOWEL DIGRAPHS

SPELLING THE SOUND /oi/ with *oi, oy*

oil	boy
toy	joy
soil	join
boil	point

WORD CARDS FOR THE VOWEL DIGRAPHS

SPELLING THE SOUND /oi/ with *oi, oy*

moist	enjoy
spoil	oyster
coin	foil
broil	pointer

SPELLING-THE-SOUND SHEET

The Vowel Digraph /oo/ with *oo, ew, u–consonant–e*

moon   _____ _____ _____

flew   _____ _____ _____

June   _____ _____ _____ e

roof   _____ _____ _____

soon   _____ _____ _____

crew   _____ _____ _____

tooth   _____ _____ _____

stew   _____ _____ _____

chute   _____ _____ _____ e

flute   _____ _____ _____ _____ e

broom   _____ _____ _____

stool   _____ _____ _____ _____

WORD CARDS FOR THE VOWEL DIGRAPHS

SPELLING THE SOUND /oo/(moon) with *oo, ew, u–consonant–e*

moon	flew
June	root
soon	crew
tooth	chute

WORD CARDS FOR THE VOWEL DIGRAPHS

SPELLING THE SOUND /oo/ (moon) with *oo, ew, u–consonant–e*

flute	stew
broom	stool
roof	bloom
blew	chew

SPELLING-THE-SOUND SHEET
The Sound Chunk /air/ with *air, are, ere*

air   _____

care   _____   _____

bare   _____   _____

there   _____   _____

hair   _____   _____

dare   _____   _____

fair   _____   _____

chair   _____   _____

pair   _____   _____

stair   _____   _____   _____

spare   _____   _____   _____

airport   _____   _____   _____   _____

WORD CARDS FOR THE VOWEL DIGRAPHS

SPELLING THE SOUND CHUNK /air/ with *air, are, ere*

air	care
bare	there
hair	dare
fair	chair

WORD CARDS FOR THE VOWEL DIGRAPHS

SPELLING THE SOUND CHUNK /air/ with *air, are, ere*

pair	airport
stair	spare
share	fare
stare	airway

SPELLING-THE-SOUND SHEET

The Sound Chunk /ear/ with *ear, eer, ier*

ear   _____

near   _____   _____

deer   _____   _____

cheer   _____   _____

tear   _____   _____

fear   _____   _____

rear   _____   _____

pier   _____   _____

clear   _____   _____   _____

steer   _____   _____   _____

career   _____   _____   _____   _____

dreary   _____   _____   _____   _____

WORD CARDS FOR THE VOWEL DIGRAPHS

SPELLING THE SOUND CHUNK /ear/ with *ear, eer, ier*

ear	near
deer	cheer
tear	fear
rear	clear

WORD CARDS FOR THE VOWEL DIGRAPHS

SPELLING THE SOUND CHUNK /ear/ with *ear, eer, ier*

pier	steer
career	dreary
eerie	hear
dear	jeer

Name _____

Date _____

SPELLING-SOUNDS SORTING MAT FOR THE SOUND _____

For Lessons 3.2, 3.3, 3.4, and 3.5

Appendixes

STORY STARTERS AND RIDDLES

A

Story starter: Say to the students, "Imagine you are walking through an orchard. There are trees all around. You take a deep breath and smell apples. You look up in the tree (point) and say, "There's an a, a, apple."

Riddle: Say to the students, "I'm thinking of a word that begins with the (short-vowel) sound /a/."

I have a very sharp blade. I have a long, wooden handle. I am a tool used to chop down trees. What am I? (ax)

I am round. I am red. I am a fruit. What am I? (apple)

I am an insect. I am usually black or brown. I make and live in hills. What am I? (ant)

I fly in a rocket. Some people call me a spaceman. What am I? (astronaut)

B

Story starter: Say to the students, "Imagine you are at the playground and you see a group of your friends. You run over to see them. One of your friends tosses a ball to you. You b, b, bounce the ball."

Riddle: Say to the students, "I'm thinking of a word that begins with the sound /b/."

I am round. You can bounce me. You can catch me. What am I? (ball)

I have two beautiful wings. I was once a caterpillar. I am very colorful. What am I? (butterfly)

Monkeys like to eat me. I am yellow. I am a fruit. What am I? (banana)

I float in the water. People take rides in me. Sometimes I have a sail. What am I? (boat)

I have a beak. I like to chirp. I have two wings, and I fly through the air. What am I? (bird)

C

Story starter: Say to the students, "Imagine you are lying in bed feeling sick with a cold. Your mom comes into your room and asks how you are feeling. You try to say something, but all you can do is c, c, cough."

Riddle: Say to the students, "I'm thinking of a word that begins with the sound /c/."

I spin a cocoon. I like to crawl along a tree branch. I turn into a butterfly. What am I? (caterpillar)

I have a funny face. I have a big red nose. I like to make people laugh. What am I? (clown)

I like to meow. I like to drink milk. I am a pet. What am I? (cat)

I taste like peppermint. I have red and white stripes. I am shaped like a hook. What am I? (candy cane)

I am orange. I am a vegetable and grow under the ground. Rabbits like to eat me. What am I? (carrot)

D

Story starter: Say to the students, "Imagine you are putting on your bathing suit. You go outside to your pool and climb up to the top of the diving board. You put your arms over your head, lean over, and d, d, dive."

Riddle: Say to the students, "I'm thinking of a word that begins with the sound /d/."

You knock on me or ring my bell. I am at the front of your house. You turn my knob to open me. What am I? (door)

I am a piece of clothing. Girls might wear me when they get dressed up. I can have buttons, zippers, or bows. What am I? (dress)

I am shaped like a cube. I have dots on each side. You use me to play games. What am I? (a pair of dice)

I am round, and I have a hole in the middle. You can eat me. I can have sprinkles or frosting. What am I? (doughnut)

My name is Brontosaurus. I am very, very, big. I lived long, long, ago. What am I? (dinosaur)

E

Story starter: Say to the students, "Imagine you are in the wilds of Africa. Suddenly, the ground begins to shake as a giant animal walks toward you. You turn around and see your pet elephant, Ellie. Ellie is so happy to see you that she waves her trunk (students swing arms in front of their bodies) and says, e, e, elephant."

Riddle: Say to the students, "I'm thinking of a word that begins with the (short-vowel) sound /e/."

I am part of your arm. You can bend me. Sometimes I am called the "funny bone." What am I? (elbow)

I am a large, gray animal. I have big, floppy ears. I have a long, gray trunk. What am I? (elephant)

I am a box to ride in if you don't want to walk up or down the stairs. I have big doors that open and close. You can press my buttons. What am I? (elevator)

I am small, round, and white. You can crack me open and scramble me. Hens lay me. What am I? (egg)

F

Story starter: Say to the students, "Imagine it is a very hot day. You are so hot, you need something to cool you off. You open your drawer and find a piece of paper. You fold it forwards and backwards and make a f, f, fan."

Riddle: Say to the students, "I'm thinking of a word that begins with the sound /f/."

I cover a bird's body. I keep birds warm. I can tickle you. What am I? (feather)

I live in a pond. I am green. I like to hop on lily pads. What am I? (frog)

I swim in the water. I have a tail and fins. Sometimes I am gold. What am I? (fish)

I grow in your garden. I have a beautiful smell. You can pick me and put me in a vase. What am I? (flower)

I sit on the table with a knife and spoon. You use me to eat cake. I am shiny and silver. What am I? (fork)

G

Story starter: Say to the students, "Imagine you are getting ready to ride Goldie. You put on your riding pants, helmet, and your riding boots. You go out to the stable, and say, 'Good morning, Goldie.' You put the saddle on Goldie, put one foot in the stirrup and swing over your other leg. You go for a g, g, gallop on Goldie."

Riddle: Say to the students, "I'm thinking of a word that begins with the sound /g/."

Some people wear me so that they can see better. I have round or square frames. I am made out of glass or plastic. What am I? (glasses)

I am fruit. I can be green, red, or purple. I grow in clusters. I am small and round. What am I? (grapes)

I am an animal that you might see at the zoo. I come from the forests of Africa. I look like a big monkey. What am I? (gorilla)

I cover your fingers. You wear me in the winter. I keep your hands warm. What am I? (gloves)

I am green. You can have a picnic on me. I am cut with a lawnmower. What am I? (grass)

H

Story starter: Say to the students, "Imagine your friend called you. You pick up the phone, and your friend says, 'Why did the hippo cross the road? Because he wanted to hop to the other side.' You put your hand in front of your mouth and say, h, h, h."

Riddle: Say to the students, "I'm thinking of a word that begins with the sound /h/."

People live inside me. I have windows and doors. I have bedrooms, a bathroom, and a kitchen. What am I? (house)

I am red. You think of "love" when you see me. What am I? (heart)

You use me to put nails into wood. I make a loud noise when you use me. I am found in a toolbox. What am I? (hammer)

I have five fingers. You use me to pick up cookies. You use me to print your name. What am I? (hand)

I am long and shaped like a tube. Water comes out of my nozzle. I am used to water the grass. What am I? (hose)

I

Story starter: Say to the students, "Imagine you wake up one morning and look in the mirror. You have red spots all over your body. Oh no! You have the chicken pox. You i, i, itch all over."

Riddle: Say to the students, "I'm thinking of a word that begins with the (short-vowel) sound /i/."

I am black or blue. I am found inside a pen. I make the marks on a paper. What am I? (ink)

I am another name for bug. I have six legs. I can crawl or fly. What am I? (insect)

I am a house. I am made out of ice blocks. I am round and white. What am I? (igloo)

I am a reptile. I am green with a long tail. I am a large lizard. What am I? (iguana)

J

Story starter: Say to the students, "Imagine you are in the gym. Your teacher leads the exercises. You touch your toes ten times and run on the spot. You j, j, jump up and down."

Riddle: Say to the students, "I'm thinking of a word that begins with the sound /j/."

I am a sea animal. I have long tentacles. I am clear and look like jelly. What am I? (jellyfish)

I am a toy. I live in a box. You wind me up and I will pop out and surprise you. What am I? (jack-in-the-box)

I may be made out of gold or silver. I can be earrings or necklaces or rings. What am I? (jewelry)

I have a pouring spout and a handle. You can keep apple juice in me. I rhyme with mug. What am I? (jug)

I have a lid. I am made out of glass. You can keep mayonnaise, mustard, or insects in me. What am I? (jar)

Story Starters and Riddles

K

Story starter: Say to the students, "Imagine you are at karate school. You put on your black belt and get ready to practice. You put your hands in front of you and k, k, karate chop."

Riddle: Say to the students, "I'm thinking of a word that begins with the sound /k/."

I am an animal. My baby lives in my pouch and his name is Joey. I like to hop. What am I? (kangaroo)

I am a man. I wear a crown. I rule a country. What am I? (king)

I lock a door. I am found on a small chain. You fit me into a keyhole. What am I? (key)

I am made out of paper, string, and a wood frame. On a windy day I fly high in the sky. I rhyme with night. What am I? (kite)

I am a baby cat. I like to lick my paws. I like to purr. What am I? (kitten)

L

Story starter: Say to the students, "Imagine you are going for a ride in the car. As you pass by a store, you point and ask your dad if you may go to the store. You go inside, buy a lollipop, and l, l, lick it."

Riddle: Say to the students, "I'm thinking of a word that begins with the sound /l/."

I am part of your doorknob. You need a key to use me. I keep your home safe. I rhyme with sock. What am I? (lock)

I am an insect. I am red with black dots. I will fly away if you touch me. What am I? (ladybug)

You put a light bulb in me. I light up a room. I wear a shade. What am I? (lamp)

You climb up me. I lean against the side of your house when you use me. I have rungs. What am I? (ladder)

You find me on a tree. I am green, but I can turn red. Sometimes I fall off the tree in the autumn. What am I? (leaf)

M

Story starter: Say to the students, "Imagine you live on a farm. You get up early one day. You get ready and go out to the barn. You find your stool and bucket and sit down to m, m, milk Mabel."

Riddle: Say to the students, "I'm thinking of a word that begins with the sound /m/."

I hold the mail. People put birthday cards and letters in me when they want to mail them to their family and friends. What am I? (mailbox)

I am a small gray animal. I like to eat cheese. I don't like to get caught in a trap. What am I? (mouse)

I am used to dust the floor. I have a long handle. I rhyme with hop. What am I? (mop)

I cover your hands. I keep them warm. I am made out of wool. What am I? (mittens)

I might be round or crescent-shaped. I shine in the night sky. I rhyme with *soon*. What am I? (moon)

N

Story starter: Say to the students, "Imagine you are sitting at the dinner table. Your mom passes you some of your favorite noodles. You spoon out a big helping. Your sister passes you some spinach. You tell her, 'N,n, no thank you!'"

Riddle: Say to the students, "I'm thinking of a word that begins with the sound /n/."

I am made out of steel. I need a hammer to put me into wood. I keep pieces of wood together. What am I? (nail)

Your mom and dad like to read me every day. I have large pages. I am black and white. What am I? (newspaper)

Sometimes fish get caught in me. I have a long pole. You also use me to catch butterflies. What am I? (net)

I have a shell. You have to crack me open to eat me. Squirrels like to store me away for the winter. What am I? (nut)

I am long, thin, and sharp. You use me to sew clothes. You put a piece of thread through my eye. What am I? (needle)

O

Story starter: Say to the students, "Imagine you are going for a swim. You put on your face mask, flippers, and oxygen tank. You dive under the water and see an o, o, octopus waving its tentacles."

Riddle: Say to the students, "I'm thinking of a word that begins with the (short-vowel) sound /o/."

I am a bird, but I cannot fly. I have a very long neck. I bury my head in the sand when I am scared. What am I? (ostrich)

I am an animal with shiny, sleek fur. I love to swim and play. I rhyme with *hotter*. What am I?

I live underwater. I have eight legs. I spray ink when I am in danger. What am I? (octopus)

P

Story starter: Say to the students, "Imagine you are going to a movie and you buy your ticket. You go to the snack bar and you watch the popcorn machine making p, p, popcorn."

Riddle: Say to the students, "I'm thinking of a word that begins with the sound /p/."

I am a piece of fruit. I am yellow or green. I rhyme with bear. What am I? (pear)

I am circular. I have pepperoni and cheese on me. You can eat me for dinner. What am I? (pizza)

I am a farm animal. I am pink. I like to say, "oink, oink." What am I? (pig)

You use me for writing. You can rub out my marks with an eraser. What am I? (pencil)

I am made out of pastry. I can be filled with fruit such as apple or cherry. I bake in the oven. What am I? (pie)

Q

Story starter: Say to the students, "Imagine you are holding your new baby brother in your arms and you rock the baby to sleep. Just then, Mom comes into the room and you say, 'The baby is asleep. Please be q, q, quiet.'"

Riddle: Say to the students, "I'm thinking of a word that begins with kw."

I am a blanket. I am made out of different pieces of material sewn together. I rhyme with built. What am I? (quilt)

I am a bird. I am related to partridges. I rhyme with *whale*. What am I? (quail)

I am a woman. I wear a crown. I rule a country. What am I? (queen)

I am shaped like a backward *S* with a dot at the bottom. When you are reading a book I tell you when there is a question. What am I? (question mark)

R

Story starter: Say to the students, "Imagine you are visiting the zoo. You walk by the biggest cage. You point to the lion and say, 'Hey look, there's R, R, Rori.'"

Riddle: Say to the students, "I'm thinking of a word that begins with the sound /r/."

You find me in the sky. I come out after it rains. I have many bright colors. What am I? (rainbow)

You wear me around your finger. I am a piece of jewelry. I can be made out of silver or gold. What am I? (ring)

You can call me a bunny. I like to eat carrots and lettuce. I like to hop around. What am I? (rabbit)

You use me to gather your leaves in a pile. I live in the garage. I have a long handle. What am I? (rake)

Babies like to shake me. I have a plastic handle. I make a noise when you move me. What am I? (rattle)

S

Story starter: Say to the students, "Imagine you have a pet snake named Sammy. You go up to your room and notice that the snake is missing. You look under the chair. No Sammy. You look in the closet. No Sammy. Then you hear, Ssss. You look under your bed, and there is S, S, Sammy."

Riddle: Say to the students, "I'm thinking of a word that begins with the sound /s/."

You wear me on your feet. You cover me with shoes or boots. I keep your feet warm. What am I? (socks)

I twinkle, twinkle in the night sky. You can make a wish on me. I rhyme with *far*. What am I?

I sit on the table next to a knife and a fork. You use me to eat soup. I am shiny and silver. What am I? (spoon)

I have eight legs. I spin a web. I like to catch and eat flies. What am I? (spider)

I am a ball of fire and gas. I shine brightly in the sky. Plants and animals need me to grow. What am I? (sun)

T

Story starter: Say to the students, "Imagine you are playing baseball in the backyard. You accidentally hit the ball near your dog Tex. Tex is sleeping so you t, t, tiptoe past Tex to get the ball."

Riddle: Say to the students, "I'm thinking of a word that begins with the sound /t/.

I am a very tall plant. I have leaves, bark, and branches. You can sit under me for shade. What am I? (tree)

I am a number. I come after the number one. I rhyme with *glue*. What am I? (two)

I am a small machine. You can dial numbers on me. You can talk into my mouthpiece. What am I? (telephone)

I have four or more wheels. I carry big loads. Sometimes I carry garbage. What am I? (truck)

I am a shape. I have three straight sides. A slice of pizza is shaped like me. What am I? (triangle)

U

Story starter: Say to the students, "Imagine you are snorkeling in the water. You swim along a beautiful coral reef. You see a school of fish, so you swim u, u, under the water. Then you swim back u, u, up to get a breath of air."

Riddle: Say to the students, "I'm thinking of a word that begins with the (short-vowel) sound /u/."

> You wear me under blue jeans or a dress. You put on a clean pair every morning. What am I? (underwear)

> You need me for a rainy day. I keep you dry. You open me up and hold me over your head. What am I? (umbrella)

> If you want to go scuba diving, you must swim in me. You dive into me. What am I? (underwater)

V

Story starter: Say to the students, "Imagine you are eating some popcorn. You accidentally spill it all over the carpet. You get the vacuum out of the closet, and v, v, vacuum the carpet."

Riddle: Say to the students, "I'm thinking of a word that begins with the sound /v/."

> I am a musical instrument. I look like a little guitar. You hold one end of me under your chin. What am I? (violin)

> My special day is February 14th. I am shaped like a heart. I am pink or red. What am I? (valentine)

> I am a container that holds water. You put flowers in me. I am made out of glass or pottery. What am I? (vase)

> Sometimes I blow my top off. Hot, red lava pours out of me. What am I? (volcano)

> I am a machine that you use to pick up the dirt from a carpet or rug. I make a noise when you turn me on. You push my handle to make me move. What am I? (vacuum cleaner)

W

Story starter: Say to the students, "Imagine you are watching a parade. A clown walks by and you wave. A funny car drives by and you wave. People in the marching band walk by and you w, w, wave to them."

Riddle: Say to the students, "I'm thinking of a word that begins with the sound /w/."

You wear me on your wrist. I can tell you the time. There are numerals on my face. What am I? (watch)

I am the largest mammal in the world. I live in the ocean. I blow water out of my blow hole. What am I? (whale)

I look like a big seal. I have two white tusks. I live in the snow and ice. What am I? (walrus)

I have four wheels and a handle. You can put your teddy bears in me and give them a ride. Sometimes your mom or dad can give you a ride in me. What am I? (wagon)

I live in your garden. I like to crawl around in dirt. If you pick me up, I wiggle. What am I? (worm)

X

Story starter: Say to the students, "Imagine you are climbing up to your tree house. There's a sign on the door that says Clubhouse. You knock on the door. Your friend opens the door and says, 'What is the password?' You make an X with your arms and say ks, ks, ks."

Riddle: Say to the students, "I'm thinking of a word that has a ks in it."

You use me to chop wood. I have a wooden handle. I have a very sharp blade. What am I? (ax)

I am a number. I come after the number five. What am I? (six)

I am shaped like a cube. You can put things in me. I am made out of cardboard. What am I? (box)

Y

Story starter: Say to the students, "Imagine you have just come home from school. You open the door, hang up your backpack, and smell freshly baked cookies. You follow the smell to the kitchen where you find your dad putting cookies in the cookie jar. Your dad asks if you would like a cookie. You nod your head, y, y, yes, and reach for a cookie."

Riddle: Say to the students, "I'm thinking of a word that begins with the sound /y/."

I am an animal. I have two horns. I rhyme with *pack*. What am I? (yak)

I am made out of wool. I look like string rolled up in a ball. You use me to knit sweaters. I rhyme with *barn*. What am I? (yarn)

When you are tired, you do this. Your mouth opens very wide. I rhyme with *dawn*. What am I? (yawn)

I am yellow. I am on the inside of an egg. You see me when you crack open my shell. What am I? (yolk)

I am a toy. I have a long piece of string tied around a round, wooden shape. You try to make me move up and down with the string. What am I? (yo-yo)

Z

Story starter: Say to the students, "Imagine you have just finished your breakfast, and you run outside to play. Suddenly, a big gust of wind blows, and you shiver. You run back into the house for your jacket, put it on, and z, z, zip it up."

Riddle: Say to the students, "I'm thinking of a word that begins with the sound /z/."

I am a vegetable. I am green. I look like a cucumber. What am I? (zucchini)

I am a wild animal. I look like a horse, but I have black and white stripes. Sometimes you see me at the zoo. What am I? (zebra)

I am a line that moves from side to side and up and down. What am I? (zigzag)

You use me to do up your coat. You use me to do up your jeans. You can move me up and down. What am I? (zipper)

I am a number. I come before the number one. I am shaped like an oval. What am I? (zero)

Aa

Pretend to point to an apple in a tree, while saying the (short vowel) sound /a/, /a/, /a/.

Bb

Pretend to bounce a ball, while saying the sound /b/, /b/, /b/.

Cc

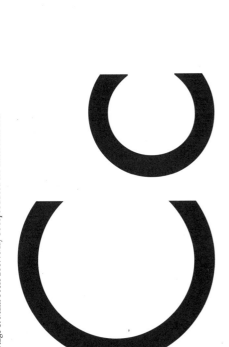

Cover your mouth and pretend to cough, while saying the sound /c/, /c/, /c/.

Dd

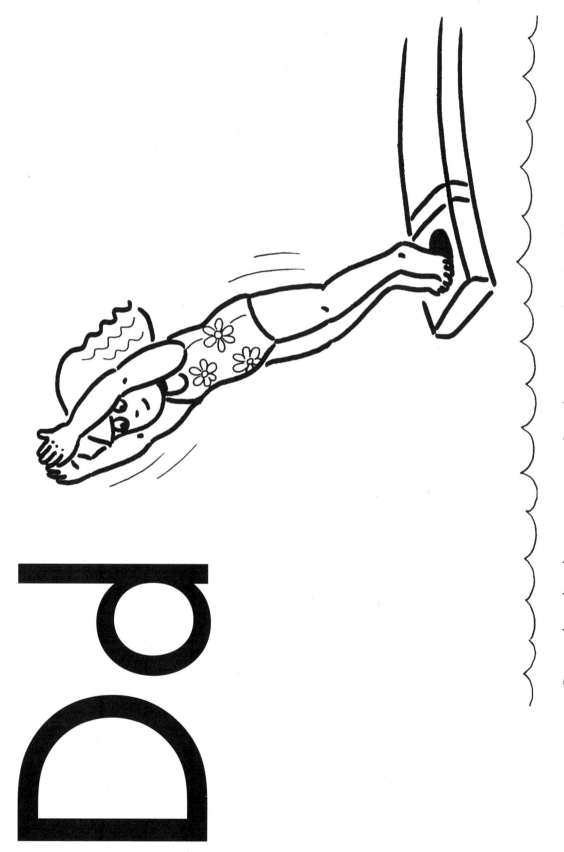

Pretend to dive by putting your hands over your head and leaning over, while saying the sound /d/, /d/, /d/.

Ee

Swing your arms and pretend they are an elephant's trunk, while saying the (short vowel) sound /e/, /e/, /e/.

Ff

Wave your hand like a fan, while saying the sound /f/, /f/, /f/.

Gg

Goldie

Pretend to gallop on Goldie, while saying the sound /g/, /g/, /g/.

Hh

Pretend to laugh, putting your hand in front of your mouth, while saying the sound /h/, /h/, /h/.

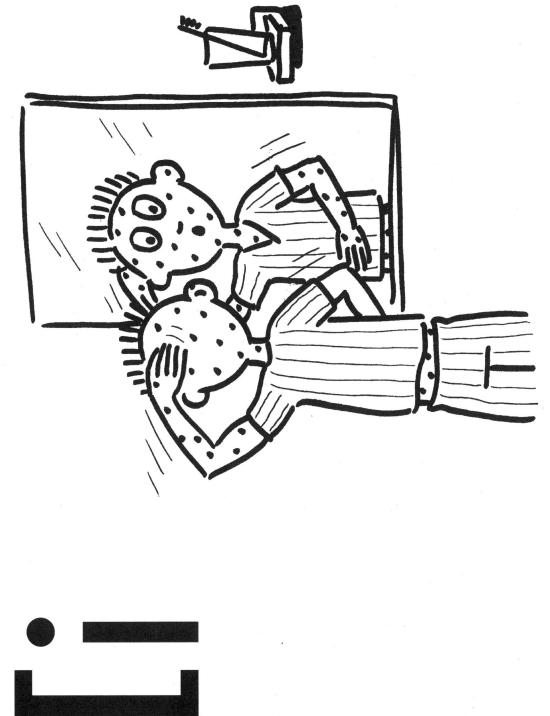

I i

Pretend to scratch all over your body, while saying the (short vowel) sound /i/, /i/, /i/.

Jj

Jump up and down, while saying the sound /j/, /j/, /j/.

Kk

Pretend to give a karate chop, while saying the sound /k/, /k/, /k/.

Pretend to lick a lollipop, while saying the sound /l/, /l/, /l/.

Mm

Pretend to milk Mabel, while saying the sound, /m/, /m/, /m/.

Nn

no!

Shake your head "no," while saying the sound /n/, /n/, /n/.

Oo

Wave your arms like the tentacles of an octopus, while saying the (short vowel) sound /o/, /o/, /o/.

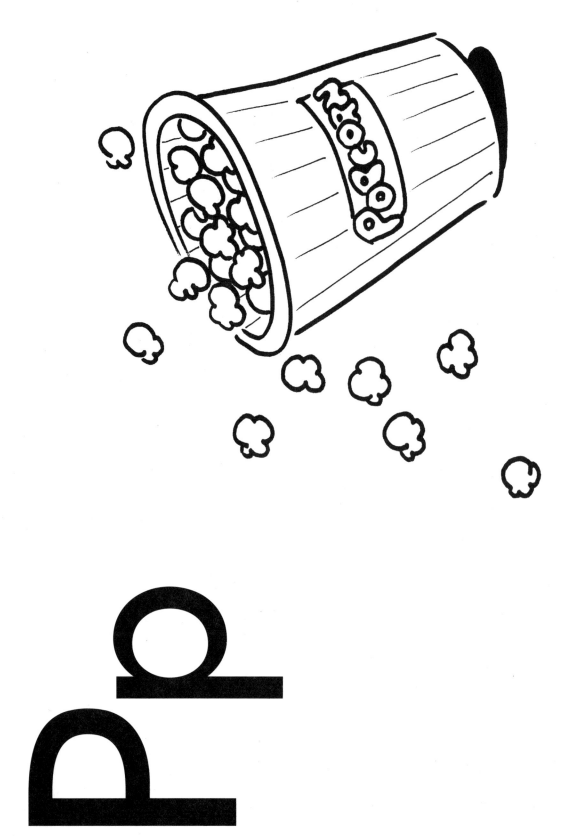

Pp

Pretend to pop up and down like popcorn, while saying the sound /p/, /p/, /p/.

Qq

Put your finger to your lips and in a quiet voice say the sound /q/, /q/, /q/.

Rr

Rorie

Pretend to roar like Rori, while making the sound /r/, /r/, /r/.

Ss

Wave your hands in the air like a snake, while saying the sound /s/, /s/, /s/.

Tt

Tiptoe around the room, while saying the sound /t/, /t/, /t/.

U u

Pretend to swim under the water, while saying the (short vowel) sound /u/, /u/, /u/.

Pretend to vacuum the carpet, while saying the sound /v/, /v/, /v/.

Pretend to wave to the people in the parade, while saying the sound /w/, /w/, /w/.

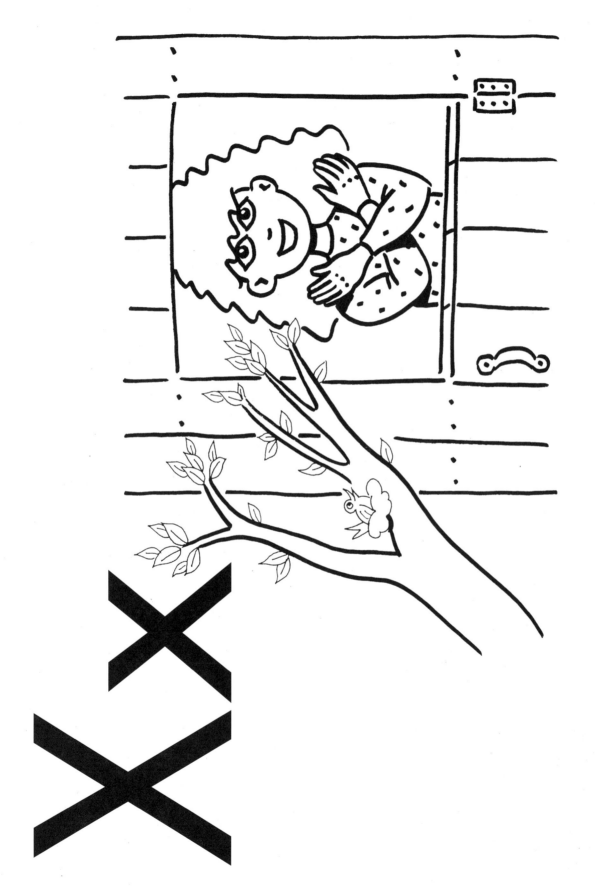

Make large Xs in the air by crossing your arms, while saying the sound /x/, /x/, /x/ (ks, ks, ks).

yes

cookies

Yy

Nod your head "yes," while saying the sound /y/, /y/, /y/.

Zz

z z z z z

Pretend to zip up a zipper, while making the sound /z/ , /z/ , /z/ .

VISUAL STRIPS FOR SOUND GROUPS A, B, C, D, AND E

VISUAL STRIPS FOR SHORT-VOWEL SOUNDS

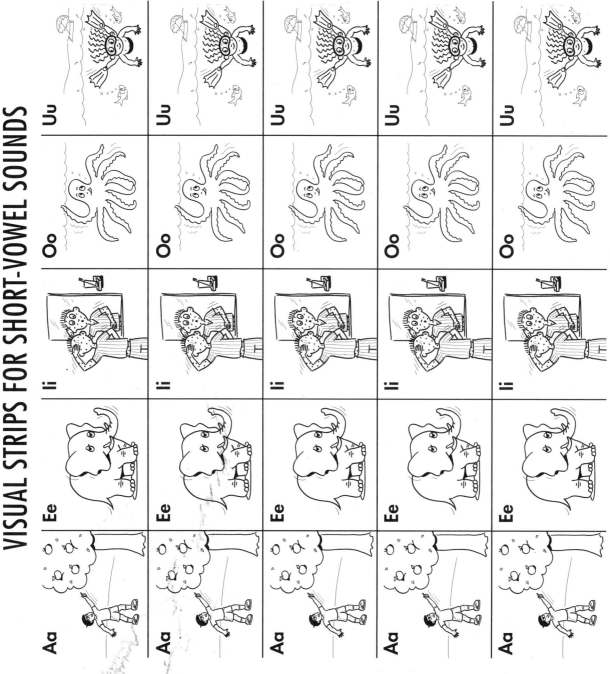

Aa   Ee   Ii   Oo   Uu

230

For Lessons 1.1 to 1.6

PICTURES PAGE FOR THE SOUND /a/

_____   _____

_____   _____

WORDS-AND-PICTURES PAGE FOR THE SOUND /a/

 ax

 apple

 ant

 astronaut

PICTURES PAGE FOR THE SOUND /b/

 _____

 _____

 _____

 _____

 _____

WORDS-AND-PICTURES PAGE FOR THE SOUND /b/

 ball

 banana

 butterfly

 boat

 bird

PICTURES PAGE FOR THE SOUND /c/

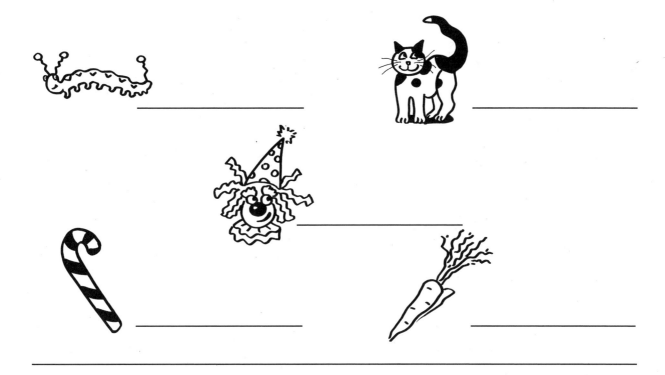

_____

_____

_____

_____

_____

WORDS-AND-PICTURES PAGE FOR THE SOUND /c/

caterpillar   cat

clown

candy cane   carrot

PICTURES PAGE FOR THE SOUND /d/

WORDS-AND-PICTURES PAGE FOR THE SOUND /d/

 door   dice

 dress

 doughnut    dinosaur

PICTURES PAGE FOR THE SOUND /e/

WORDS-AND-PICTURES PAGE FOR THE SOUND /e/

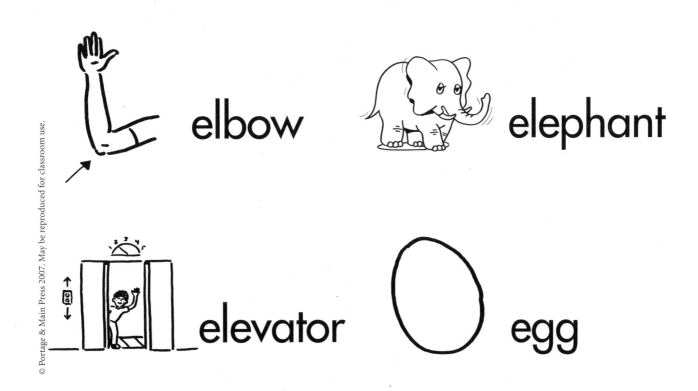

elbow

elephant

elevator

egg

PICTURES PAGE FOR THE SOUND /f/

_____

WORDS-AND-PICTURES PAGE FOR THE SOUND /f/

feather

fish

frog

flower

fork

PICTURES PAGE FOR THE SOUND /g/

_____   _____

_____

_____   _____

WORDS-AND-PICTURES PAGE FOR THE SOUND /g/

 glasses    gorilla

 grapes

 gloves   grass

PICTURES PAGE FOR THE SOUND /h/

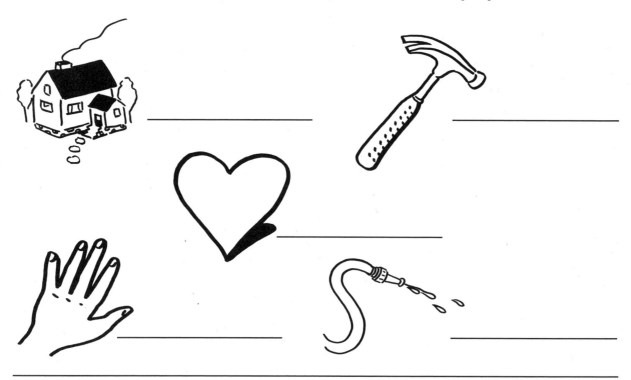

_____

_____

_____

_____

WORDS-AND-PICTURES PAGE FOR THE SOUND /h/

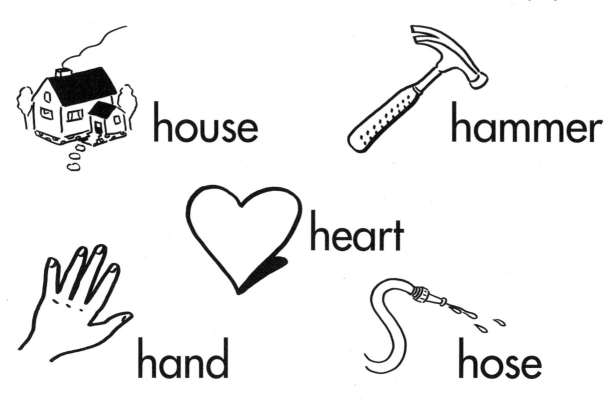

house

hammer

heart

hand

hose

PICTURES PAGE FOR THE SOUND /i/

 _____

 _____

 _____

 _____

WORDS-AND-PICTURES PAGE FOR THE SOUND /i/

 ink

 insect

 igloo

 iguana

PICTURES PAGE FOR THE SOUND /j/

WORDS-AND-PICTURES PAGE FOR THE SOUND /j/

jellyfish   jewelry

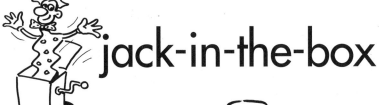

jack-in-the-box

jug

jar

PICTURES PAGE FOR THE SOUND /k/

_____   _____

_____

_____   _____

WORDS-AND-PICTURES PAGE FOR THE SOUND /k/

 kangaroo

 key

 king

 kite

 kitten

PICTURES PAGE FOR THE SOUND /l/

WORDS-AND-PICTURES PAGE FOR THE SOUND /l/

lock

lamp

ladybug

ladder

leaf

PICTURES PAGE FOR THE SOUND /m/

_____

_____

_____

_____

_____

WORDS-AND-PICTURES PAGE FOR THE SOUND /m/

 mailbox

 mop

mouse

 mittens

 moon

PICTURES PAGE FOR THE SOUND /n/

_____

_____

_____

_____

WORDS-AND-PICTURES PAGE FOR THE SOUND /n/

 nail

 net

 newspaper

 nuts

 needle

PICTURES PAGE FOR THE SOUND /o/

_____ _____

_____

WORDS-AND-PICTURES PAGE FOR THE SOUND /o/

ostrich   octopus

otter

PICTURES PAGE FOR THE SOUND /p/

_____

WORDS-AND-PICTURES PAGE FOR THE SOUND /p/

pear

pig

pizza

pencil

pie

PICTURES PAGE FOR THE SOUND /q/

WORDS-AND-PICTURES PAGE FOR THE SOUND /q/

quilt

quail

queen

question

PICTURES PAGE FOR THE SOUND /r/

WORDS-AND-PICTURES PAGE FOR THE SOUND /r/

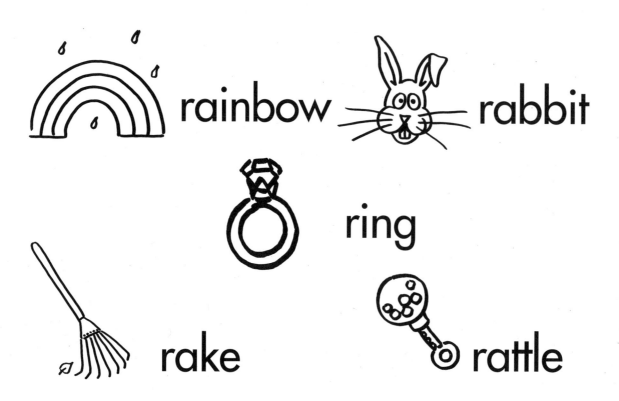

rainbow rabbit

ring

rake rattle

PICTURES PAGE FOR THE SOUND /s/

_____

_____

_____

_____

_____

WORDS-AND-PICTURES PAGE FOR THE SOUND /s/

 socks

 spoon

star

 spider

 sun

PICTURES PAGE FOR THE SOUND /t/

WORDS-AND-PICTURES PAGE FOR THE SOUND /t/

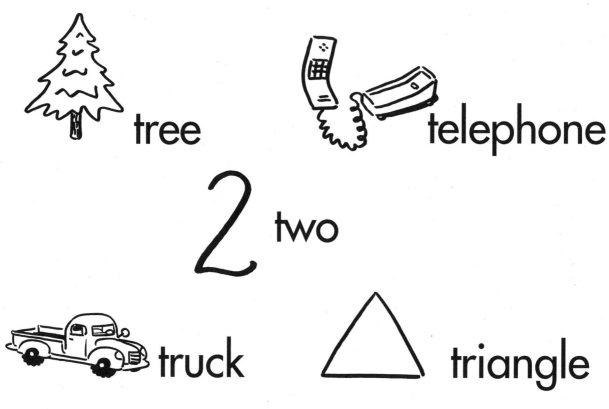

PICTURES PAGE FOR THE SOUND /u/

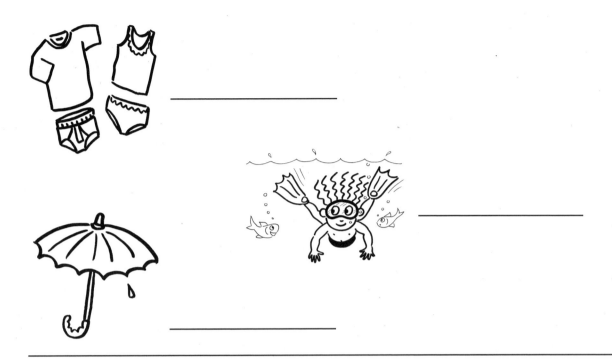

_____

_____

_____

WORDS-AND-PICTURES PAGE FOR THE SOUND /u/

 underwear

 underwater

 umbrella

PICTURES PAGE FOR THE SOUND /v/

WORDS-AND-PICTURES PAGE FOR THE SOUND /v/

violin

vase

valentine

volcano

vacuum

PICTURES PAGE FOR THE SOUND /w/

_____

_____

_____

_____

WORDS-AND-PICTURES PAGE FOR THE SOUND /w/

 watch

 walrus

 whale

 wagon

 worm

PICTURES PAGE FOR THE SOUND /x/

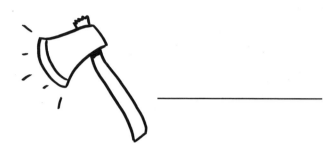 _____   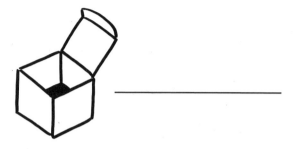 _____

6 _____

WORDS-AND-PICTURES PAGE FOR THE SOUND /x/

 ax    box

6 six

PICTURES PAGE FOR THE SOUND /y/

WORDS-AND-PICTURES PAGE FOR THE SOUND /y/

PICTURES PAGE FOR THE SOUND /z/

_____

WORDS-AND-PICTURES PAGE FOR THE SOUND /z/

zucchini   zigzag

zebra

zipper   zero

Bibliography

Adams, M.J. *Beginning to Read: Thinking and Learning about Print.* Cambridge, MA: MIT Press, 1990.

Anthony, J., and C. Lonigan. "The Nature of Phonological Awareness: Converging Evidence from Four Studies of Preschool and Early Grade School Children." *Journal of Educational Psychology* 96.1 (2004): 43–55.

Baker, S., and S. Stahl. "Beginning Reading: Educational Tools for Diverse Learners." *School Psychology of Review* 23.3 (1994): 372–95.

Ball, E.W., and B.A. Blachman. "Phoneme Segmentation Training: Effect on Reading Readiness." *Annals of Dyslexia* 38 (1988): 208–25.

_____. "Does Phoneme Awareness Training in Kindergarten Make a Difference in Early Word Recognition and Developmental Spelling?" *Reading Research Quarterly* 26 (1991): 49–66

Berninger, V.W. *Reading and Writing Acquisitions: A Developmental Neuropsychological Perspective.* Boulder, CO: Westview, 1996.

Blachman, B. "Phonological Awareness." In *Handbook of Reading Research*, vol. 3, edited by M. Kamil, P. Mosenthal, P. Pearson, and R. Barr, 483–98. Mahwah, NJ: Lawrence Erlbaum Associates, 2002.

Blachman, B. A. "Relationship of Rapid Naming Ability and Language Analysis Skills to Kindergarten and First-Grade Reading Achievement." *Journal of Educational Psychology* 76 (1984): 610–22.

Bond, G.L., and R. Dykstra. "The Cooperative Research Program in First-Grade Reading Instruction." *Reading Research Quarterly* 32.4 (1997): 348–427.

Bradley, L., and P.E. Bryant. "Categorizing Sounds and Learning to Read: A Causal Connection." *Nature* 301 (1983): 419–21.

Bradley, L., and P.E. Bryant. *Rhyme and Reason in Reading and Spelling.* International Academy for Research in Learning Disabilities Monograph Series, No. 1. Ann Arbor: University of Michigan Press, 1985.

Bursuck, W., D. Munk, D. Nelson, and M. Curran. "Research on the Prevention of Reading Problems: Are Kindergarten and First-Grade Teachers Listening?" *Preventing School Failure* 47.1 (2002): 4–9.

Byrne, B., and R. Fielding-Barnsley. "Evaluation of a Program to Teach Phonemic Awareness to Young Children: A One-Year Follow-Up." *Journal of Educational Psychology* 85 (1993): 104–11.

Calfee, R.C., and K.A. Norman. "Psychological Perspectives on the Early Reading Wars: The Case of Phonological Awareness." *Teachers College Record* 100.2 (1998): 242–75.

Carr, E., and L. Aldinger. *Reading Works: Strategies for Learning to Read.* Toledo, OH: Thinking Works, 2001.

Catts, H., and T. Vartiainen. *Sounds Abound.* East Moline, IL: Lingui Systems, 1993.

Clay, M.M. *Becoming Literate: The Construction of Inner Control.* Portsmouth, NH: Heinemann, 1991.

Cunningham, A.E. "Explicit Versus Implicit Instruction in Phonemic Awareness." *Journal of Experimental Child Psychology* 50 (1990): 429–44.

Cunningham, P.M. *Phonics They Use: Words for Reading and Writing.* New York: HarperCollins, 1991.

Ehri, L., and S. Nunes. "The Role of Phonemic Awareness in Learning to Read." In *What Research Has to Say about Reading Instruction*, edited by A. Farstrup and S. Samuels, 110–39. Newark, DE: International Reading Association, 2002.

Flesch, R. *Why Johnny Can't Read and What You Can Do about It.* New York: Harper and Brothers, 1955.

Foorman, B. "Research on the Great Debate: Code-Oriented Versus Whole-Language Approaches to Reading Instruction." *School Psychology Review* 24.3 (1995): 376–42.

Foorman, B., D. Chen, C. Carlson, L. Moats, D. Francis, and J. Fletcher. "The Necessity of the Alphabetic Principle to Phonemic Awareness Instruction." *Reading and Writing: An Interdisciplinary Journal* 16 (2003): 289–324.

Goswami, U. "Phonological and Lexical Processes." In *Handbook of Reading Research*, vol. 3, edited by M. Kamil, P. Mosenthal, P. Pearson, and R. Barr, 251–67. Mahwah, NJ: Lawrence Erlbaum Associates, 2002.

Griffith, P., and M. Olson. "Phonemic Awareness Helps Beginning Readers Break the Code." *The Reading Teacher* 45.7 (1992): 516–23.

Hulme, C. "Phonemes, Rimes and the Mechanisms of Early Reading Development." *Journal of Experimental Child Psychology* 82 (2002): 58–64.

Hulme, C., P. Hatcher, K. Nation, A. Brown, J. Adams, and G. Stuart. "Phoneme Awareness Is a Better Predictor of Early Reading Skills than Onset-Rime Awareness." *Journal of Experimental Child Psychology* 82.1 (2002): 2–28.

Hurford, D.P., M. Johnston, P. Nepote, S. Hampton, S. Moore, J. Neal, A. Mueller, K. McGeorge, L. Huff, A. Awad, C. Tatro, C. Juliano, and D. Huffman. "Early Identification and Remediation of Phonological-Processing Deficits in First-Grade Children at Risk for Reading Disabilities." *Journal of Educational Psychology* 27.10 (1994): 647–59.

Jerger, M. "Phonemic Awareness and the Role of the Educator." *Intervention in School and Clinic* 32.1 (1996): 5–13.

Juel, C., P.L. Griffith, and R.B. Gough. "Acquisition of Literacy: A Longitudinal Study of Children in the First and Second Grade." *Journal of Educational Psychology* 78 (1986): 243–55.

Kenny, H.A., and L.A. Robbins. *Phonics in Action: A Balanced Early Literacy Program*. Winnipeg: Portage and Main, 1999.

Lewkowicz, N.K. "Phonemic Awareness Training: What to Teach and How to Teach It." *Journal of Educational Psychology* 72 (1980): 686–700.

Liberman, I.Y., and D. Shankweiler. "Phononology and Beginning Reading: A Tutorial." In *Learning to Read: Basic Research and its Implications*, edited by L. Rieben and C.A. Perfetti. Hillsdale, NJ: L. Erlbaum Associates (1991): 3–17.

Liberman, I.Y., D. Shankweiler, F.W. Fischer, and B. Carter. "Explicit Syllable and Phoneme Segmentation in the Young Child." *Journal of Experimental Child Psychology* 18 (1974): 201–12.

Lie, A. "Effects of a Training Program for Stimulating Skills in Word Analysis in First-Grade Children." *Reading Research Quarterly* 26.3 (1991): 234–50.

Lundberg, I., J. Frost, and O. Petersen. "Effects of an Extensive Program for Stimulating Phonological Awareness in Preschool Children." *Reading Research Quarterly* 23 (1998): 263–84.

Martin, M., and B. Byrne. "Teaching Children to Recognize Rhyme Does Not Directly Promote Phonemic Awareness." *British Journal of Educational Psychology* 72 (2002): 561–72.

McCutchen, D., R. Abbott, L. Green, S. Beretvas, S. Cox, N. Potter, T. Quiroga, and A. Gray. "Beginning Literacy: Links among Teacher Knowledge, Teacher Practice, and Student Learning." *Journal of Learning Disabilities* 35.1 (2002): 69–86.

McGuinness, C., and G. McGuinness. *Reading Reflex: The Foolproof Phono-Graphix Method for Teaching Your Child to Read.* New York: Simon and Schuster, 1998.

McGuinness, D. *Why Our Children Can't Read and What We Can Do about It.* New York: Simon and Schuster, 1997.

McGuinness, D., J. Donohue, and C. McGuinness. "Phonological Training and the Alphabet Principle: Evidence for Reciprocal Causality." *Reading Research Quarterly* 3 (1995): 830–52.

Moats, L. *Teaching Reading is Rocket Science: What Expert Teachers of Reading Should Know and Be Able to Do.* Report No. HD30995, ERIC Document Reproduction Service No. ED445323. Washington, DC: American Federation of Teachers, 1999.

Moats, L.C. *Speech to Print: Language Essentials for Teachers.* Baltimore, MD: Paul H. Brookes, 2001.

National Institute of Child Health and Human Development. *Teaching Children to Read: An Evidence-Based Assessment of the Scientific Literature on Reading and its Implications for Reading Instruction: Reports of the Subgroups.* National Institute of Health Pub. No. 00-4754. Washington, DC: U.S. Government Printing Office, 2000.

Norris, J., and P. Hoffman. "Phonemic Awareness: A Complex Developmental Process." *Topics in Language Disorders* 22.2 (2002): 1–34.

O'Connor, R.E., J.R. Jenkins, and N. Leister. "Teaching Phonological Awareness to Young Children with Learning Disabilities." *Exceptional Children* 590 (1993): 532–46.

Perfetti, C.A., I. Beck, and L. Bell. "Phonemic Knowledge and Learning to Read are Reciprocal: A Longitudinal Study of First-Grade Children." *Merrill-Palmer Quarterly* 33 (1987): 283–19.

Rasinski, T.V. *The Fluent Reader: Oral Reading Strategies for Building Word Recognition, Fluency, and Comprehension.* New York: Scholastic Professional Books, 2003.

Rasinski, T., N. Padak, R. Newton, and E. Newton. "Divide, Conquer, Combine, and Create: A Vocabulary Learning Routine for Grades 3-8." Presentation at The International Reading Association's 52nd Annual Convention, Toronto, May 2007.

Richards, R.G. *The Source for Dyslexia and Dysgraphia.* East Moline, IL: Lingui Systems, 1999.

Richgels, D.J., L.M. McGee, and K. Poremba. "Kindergartners Talk about Print: Phonemic Awareness in Meaningful Contexts." *The Reading Teacher* 49 (1996): 632–42.

Rosner, J., and D.P. Simon. "The Auditory Analysis Test: An Initial Report." ERIC ED051253, 1970.

Scheffler, A., M. Richmond, and R. Kazelskis. "Examining Shifts in Teachers' Theoretical Orientations to Reading." *Reading Psychology: An International Quarterly* 14.1 (1993): 1–13.

Share, D.L., A.F. Jorm, R. Maclean, and R. Matthews. "Sources of Individual Differences in Reading Acquisition." *Journal of Educational Psychology* 76 (1984): 1 309–24.

Snider, V.E. "A Primer on Phonemic Awareness: What It Is, Why It's Important, and How to Teach It." *School of Psychology Review* 24.3 (1995): 443–45.

_____. "The Relationship between Phonemic Awareness and Later Reading Achievement." *Journal of Educational Research* 90 (1997): 203–11.

Spiegel, D.L. "Blending Whole Language and Systematic Direct Instruction." *The Reading Teacher* 46 (September 1992): 38–48.

Stanovich, K.E. "Matthews Effects in Reading: Some Consequences of Individual Differences in Reading." *Reading Research Quarterly* 21 (1986): 360–407.

Stanovich, K.E., A.E. Cunningham, and D. Feeman. "Intelligence, Cognitive Skills, and Early Reading Progress." *Reading Research Quarterly* 19 (1984): 278–303.

Tunmer, W.E., and A.R. Nesdale. "Phonemic Segmentation Skill and Beginning Reading." *Journal of Educational Psychology* 77 (1985): 417–27.

Wagner, R.K., and J.K. Torgesen. "The Nature of Phonological Processing and its Causal Role in the Acquisition of Reading Skills." *Psychology Bulletin* 101.2 (1987): 192–212.

Wagner, R.K., J.K. Torgesen, and C.A. Rashotte. "Development of Reading-Related Phonological Processing Abilities: New Evidence of Bi-Directional Causality from a Latent Variable Longitudinal Study." *Developmental Psychology* 30 (1994): 73–87.

Yopp, H.K. "The Validity and Reliability of Phonemic Awareness Tests." *Reading Research Quarterly* 23 (1988): 159–77.

_____. "Developing Phonemic Awareness in Young Children." *The Reading Teacher* 45 (May 1992): 696–703.

_____. "A Test for Assessing Phonemic Awareness in Young Children." *The Reading Teacher* 49 (1995): 20–29.

Yopp, H., and R. Yopp. "Supporting Phonemic Awareness Development in the Classroom." *The Reading Teacher* 54.2 (2000): 130–43.